COSMIC BIBLE

Paradigm Revolution
by Paradoxical Truth

BOOK 2

Minoru Uba

Copyright © 2015 by Minoru Uba

COSMIC BIBLE BOOK 2

Published by Babel Press U.S.A.
All rights reserved.
Date of publication: May 21, 2015

This book was originally published in Japanese under the title "宇宙聖書" by VOICE, Japan in 2010.

Author: Minoru Uba

Director: Tomoki Hotta

Original translation by Self-Healing Study and Practice Group
Edited and translated by Gyoko Koike

Coordinator: Junko Rodriguez
Formatting: Sota Torigoe

ISBN: 978-0989232630

Babel Corporation
Pacific Business News Bldg. #208,
1833 Kalakaua Avenue,
Honolulu, Hawaii 96815

Phone: (808) 946 - 3773
Fax: (808) 946 - 3993

Website: http://www.bookandright.com/

CONTENTS

Chapter Two ☆ The Deriving Point

2-1. The existence purpose of consciousness and existence value of individuality…..11
2-2. Formation process of consciousness based on the personality formation history…..12
2-3. Formation process of consciousness and the three elements…..14
2-4. Verifying the "Cluster" of spiritual consciousness entity…..16
2-5. "Original existence consciousnesses" are the primordial consciousness of terrestrial life…..18
2-6. Formation process of "original existence consciousnesses" and the two elements…..19
2-7. Transitions of "instinctive survival consciousnesses" in history…..20
2-8. The terrestrial life has common desire consciousness and performs common ecological action…..23
2-9. Spiritual evolution is the release from "instinctive survival consciousnesses"…..25
2-10. Sexual maturity and spiritual evolution…..27
2-11. Release of undifferentiated sexual desire consciousness and spiritual evolution…..29
2-12. Subconscious is derived from the physical and spiritual formation history…..33
2-13. "Reincarnation consciousness" is the direct subconscious…..34
2-14. "Genetic consciousness" is the indirect subconscious…..35
2-15. The fundamental difference between subconscious of the soul and the body…..37
2-16. Law of causality in Buddhism theory is untruth…..38

2-17. Genetic linkage and reincarnation are both related to the principle of Self-responsibility…..42
2-18. Emerging consciousnesses are formed in two stages…..44
2-19. The purpose of the personality formation and the physical body formation in the prenatal life…..45
2-20. Ideal personality formation in the prenatal life…..45
2-21. Taboos of personality formations in the womb…..47
2-22. Ideal physical formation in the prenatal life…..48
2-23. Taboos of physical formation in the prenatal life…..49
2-24. Womb is a sanctuary for "change by birth and re-birth"…..50
2-25. Womb is a sanctuary for physical evolution…..51
2-26. Womb is a sanctuary of spiritual evolution…..56
2-27. Personality formation based on the earth environment…..60
2-28. The existing purpose and the existing value in the earth life…..60
2-29. Earth life determines the spiritual dimension…..63
2-30. Ideal personality formation in the earth life…..67
2-31. Emotional relationship between child and parents, and the "rule of relativity"…..68
2-32. The ideal family of love, which cannot be built with religion or philosophy…..70
2-33. Emerging consciousnesses and the importance of maternal love…..77
2-34. Emerging consciousnesses is the final chapter of consciousness formation…..79
2-35. Time axis domination by the brain memory…..79
2-36. Human history is a journey of Self-discovery…..81
2-37. Acquisition competition for the evaluation by others and integration disorder…..82
2-38. The existence of SHINSEI, which is the root consciousness …..83

2-39. True inherent nature existing in the root consciousness…..86
2-40. Limits of the material world on the time axis…..88
2-41. The basic principle of the Universe…..90
2-42. Relative subject and the "principles of dimensional integration"…..93
2-43. Relative object and the "principle of dimensional domination"…..94
2-44. The "rule of the relative original power" based on the "rule of balance"…..96
2-45. Life creation process on the earth star…..98
2-46. The earth star is a unique planet…..100
2-47. Mathematical evaluation leads to competition and domination…..102
2-48. Words and languages are specific presence on the earth star…..103
2-49. The earth star performs the role and responsibilities of a prison planet…..105
2-50. The "rule of give and take" on the earth star…..107
2-51. The "rule of give and give" of the universe…..108
2-52. Prison in the prison star (earth) is a geriatric hospital…..110
2-53. The degree of freedom of consciousness and the degree of acceptance of love based on spiritual dimension…..112
2-54. Energy wave level in the spiritual dimension…..115
2-55. Earth logic is legalized by the principle of domination…..118
2-56. Environmental adaptation is a driving force for evolution…..121
2-57. Wisdom and desire is a bipolar structure of the brain…..122
2-58. Science civilizations lead spiritual culture…..124
2-59. The universe is penetrated by the principle of integration…..127
2-60. Now is the era when the Christian Bible, Buddhist writings, and other scriptures begin to fade…..131

2-61. The earth star is filled with delusions and illusions by supposition and speculation…..133
2-62. Religion will become archaic and fade away…..135
2-63. Sexual desires cannot be released by religion…..137
2-64. The 21st century plunges into the era of ending the prison star…..143
2-65. The crisis can be avoided by liberation from religious curse…..145
2-66. Religious struggles are the common crisis of the earth star…..149
2-67. The Old Testament is the genealogy of genetic linkage from Eve…..150
2-68. The core of ONSHU of Judaism and Islam…..153
2-69. The "rule of sorrow and ONSHU in the triangle relationship" that happened in Abraham's family…..157
2-70. Great virtues of unselfishness by Self-sacrifice…..161
2-71. Analysis of personality formation history of Adolf Hitler…..166
2-72. The "rule of sorrow and ONSHU in the triangle relationship" in Jacob's family…..181
2-73. Trial and persecution produce spiritual evolution and prosperity…..182
2-74. Love and ONSHU are inherited by sentiments of women…..183
2-75. Love pillage by King David and ONSHU of Uriah…..186
2-76. Analysis of the personality formation history of Jesus Christ…..187
2-77. Historical lessons in the Bible…..191

Chapter 2

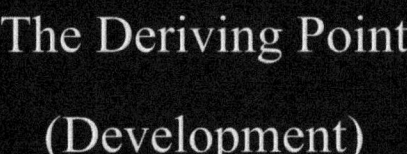

The Deriving Point

(Development)

Chapter Two ☆ The Deriving Point

2-1. The existence purpose of consciousness and the existence value of individuality

For all cause and subjectivity, the power of cause is derived from *the relative wave in the spiritual dimension and the "rule of the relative original power,"* and as a result of exercising consciousness, it forms words and deeds according to motivation based on the will.

The purpose of life and action is based on the spiritual consciousness entity of integrated spiritual dimension, which is the mental disposition according to the spirituality formation history (the subconscious of each person), and the personality according to the personality formation history (the emerging consciousness of each person). That subconscious and emerging consciousness are exercised and directed by the individuality, and then form words and deeds. The individuality is the art of consciousness which allows a person to manifest one's own happiness.

It is not possible to make any action without purpose, and there is no action without motivation. In other words, there can be no motivation or action without exercising consciousness. For example, if you deal with a person of good character, your higher consciousness will invoke and act based on the motivation of goodness. On the other hand, if you are involved with a person of unsavory character, your negative consciousness will invoke and act based on the motivation of evil. The theoretical framework of invoking a potential personality and acting based on motivation by the relativity of consciousness is an important concept of the PARAREVO theory.

Consciousness is formed based on the experience and environment, so there is no formation of consciousness without environment and no formation of consciousness without experience.

2-2. Formation process of consciousness based on the personality formation history

Personality is built by the formation process of consciousness and is largely developed by the experience based on the environment of the personality formation history.

I could say that they are formed by five major environmental experiences which are experiences based on a family environment, natural environment, social environment, cultural environment, and evolutional environment.

First, the greatest influence in our consciousness formation is the personality formation history in the family environment. The core of love and ONSHU are formed according to what kind of family environment a person is born to and grows up in. The environment and the experience of living and growing in, that environment are very important in determining the spiritual dimension, which is the heart of the consciousness structure. For example, the personality formation history of a person who was born to poor parents in a lower spiritual dimension and grew up in a horrible family environment with a lack of love will be totally different in the consciousness formation, from the personality formation history of a person who was born to parents with abundant love in a higher spiritual dimension and grew up in a family environment rich with sensibility and filled with gratitude and happiness.

Secondly, different personality formation is built on the experiences based on the natural environment. So the consciousness formation will be totally different between a person living in an area like the northern provinces, where the weather is severe and there is little sunlight, and a person living in a tropical region where the weather is warm and there is lots of bright sunshine, like in the southern provinces. For example, the incidence rates of depression and the number of suicides are much higher in the northern areas.

Thirdly, different experiences based on the various social environments build different personality formation. The consciousness formation will be totally different between a person living in a poor environment such as a revolutionary and war torn country, and a person living in a society of calmness and energy with peace and prosperity. In recent years, after the unification of East and West Germany in 1989, it has been proven that the consciousness built the personality formation in a twisted and distorted social structure between the liberal society and the communist society, is much different in the degree of freedom and the way of consciousness even though they were the same ethnic groups.

Fourthly, different experiences based on the various cultural environments build different personality formation. The motive power which forms each culture, is determined by the fundamental power of the believer's views of each religion. Even though there are differences in the form and the subject of what they believe, the basic background of each cultural environment originated by the theoretical framework and values of religion. Every spiritual culture in the world was built under the guise of religion, and as a result, the social civilizations were built. They are known as Jewish cultural sphere, Christian cultural sphere, Muslim cultural sphere, Hindu cultural sphere, Buddhist cultural sphere, and Shamanic cultural sphere built by the Native Americans of North, Central, and South America. The undeniable fact remains that the formation processes of spiritual culture has built each social civilization and ethnic or national history, by centering each in religion, as we can see by the historical monuments such as shrines and temples, which have been preserved as a fingerprint of history.

And fifth, by the environments and experiences based on the evolution process, have had a great influence on forming the race, ethnic group and nation itself. While evolution has been achieved by environmental adaptation, the formation and transition of consciousness has been directed to a higher spiritual dimension. As a result, human beings attained humanity differentiation, separating on a large scale to black race, white race, and yellow race, and achieved each unique evolution forming the individual mental entity of each race by its environment and experience.

As you can see, throughout the expansive history of family environment, natural environment, social environment, cultural environment and evolutional environment, built up consciousness has formed the life style, the society, the culture, and the nation.

Our life is directed by a compass called consciousness, so life itself can be very different depending on how we determine the existing purpose and existing value of life, and with what kind of consciousness.

2-3. Formation process of consciousness and the three elements

In each human being, there are three different consciousnesses, and each of those comes from the formation process of the consciousness. Through the spiritual evolution and the physical evolution, the formation process of the consciousness has integrated together like a three-legged race, and has achieved an existence as a cluster of consciousness.

The formation process of consciousness has accomplished all sorts of environmental adaptations in the spiritual and the physical evolution, and achieved Self-completion as a result of Self-efforts by Self-determination and Self-responsibility according to free intention, based on the rule of "spirit is subjective and body is objective," that pushes the spiritual evolution to a higher spiritual dimension.

The size, dimension, and ability of each consciousness in the way of formation process of consciousness, are different. I will verify this using an iceberg as a metaphor. The part of the iceberg that we can see on the surface of the water obviously exists. It is liken to the newest surface of consciousness in the history of the formation process of consciousness, and is called *emerging consciousness.* There is also the unseen shape of the iceberg existing under the water, which has accumulated throughout its long history. We call this consciousness, *subconscious,* and no matter how big the iceberg is, there must be an existence of the origin of primordial ice, which was the freezing point of the ice crystal. This primordial crystal is the origin of the entire iceberg and it is also the common consciousness existing as a common denominator for the entire iceberg. We call this *"original existence consciousnesses."*

As you can see by this example, emerging consciousness, subconscious, and "original existence consciousness" are different in dimension, ability, and size, according to each formation process.

The existence purpose and existence value of the formation

process of each consciousness is directed by the environment of each period, and directed to the spiritual evolution together with the physical evolution, allowing solid matter to evolve into various races. Our history to reach to Homo sapiens exists together with consciousness, and the theoretical framework and values for a life in this world is directed and determined by degrees in the spiritual evolution in the past.

★See diagram "Iceberg of Consciousness" on P17

2-4. Verifying the "cluster" of spiritual consciousness entity

Basically, the spiritual consciousness entity is composed of a complex of three consciousnesses, the "original existence consciousness," the subconscious, and the emerging consciousness. This mergence forms the "cluster" of the entire consciousness.

These three exercise according to each dimension by the relative waves in the spiritual dimension, such as "Etheric spiritual decibel dimension" (material plane), "Astral spiritual decibel dimension" ("ghost plane") and "Mental spiritual decibel dimension" ("spirit plane"). So things called fate, destiny, and fortune will be manifested as different phenomena in your life depending on your view of purpose and values, which will be determined by what kind of dimension the consciousness connects with the relative wave.

A person with a view of value only in the physical world benefits will not progress his/her spirituality and personality in the process of the spiritual evolution, and will repeat a life dominated by desire for material things.

Iceberg of Consciosnesses

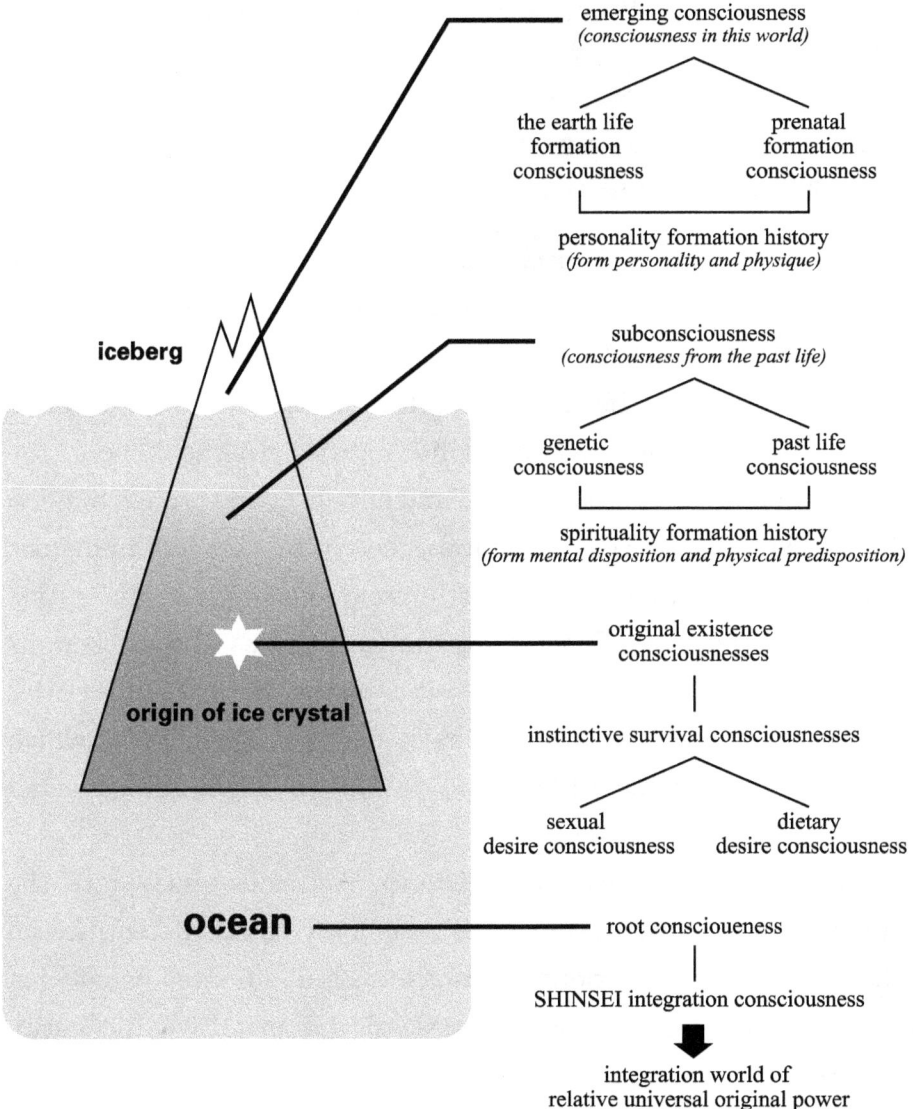

17

Therefore, unless you verify how the "cluster" which connoted in the spiritual consciousness entity, goes through the process of the formation and, becomes the aggregation of information consciousness, you are not able to discover your true self.

2-5. "Original existence consciousnesses" are the primordial consciousness of terrestrial life

If we, figuratively, talk about an iceberg as the aggregation of all living things on earth, the "original existence consciousnesses" are the first ice crystal primordially frozen, and the primordial consciousness for life entity on the earth and the common consciousnesses connoted in all life entities. In the iceberg, the various shapes of ice were created and have existed through historic environmental changes, so countless ice crystals created in history exist as life entities on the earth, from the original life entity, bacteria, to humans. Considering the various ices in an iceberg as the consciousness of various life entities on the earth, all life entities on the earth have the "original existence consciousnesses," which are liken to the primordial ice crystal, as an origin and connoted the common consciousness.

That is, if the "original existence consciousnesses" are the survival consciousnesses existing commonly in all life entities on the earth, and if *the extant consciousness* still survived, what kind of "original existence consciousnesses" did primitive life entity possess?

2-6. Formation process of "original existence consciousnesses" and the two elements

The "original existence consciousnesses" are formed by two consciousnesses. One is called *"dietary desire consciousness."* This creates essential energies for life entities to survive and be active, and exists to secure life energies to maintain the existence of life and activity. Even bacteria, the primitive life entity, have taken some sorts of energies and achieved life maintenance and activity by consuming and excreting these energies. This consciousness is the instinctive desire consciousness being fated as the essential nature (instinct) for living on the earth star.

The other is called *"sexual desire consciousness."* This consciousness exists for the preservation of species and expansion of territories. The purpose of its existence is to leave a chain of life entities to future generations. "Sexual desire consciousness" mainly performs reproductive activity, and is an instinctive desire consciousness fated to make the chain of life sustainable.

These two instinctive desire consciousnesses are collectively called the *"instinctive survival consciousnesses"* because they are the consciousnesses fated as instinctive, from primitive life entities.

The real purpose of these two major desires is directed to a common purpose. The life entities on the earth have to eat for survival. In order to eat, we have to work. In order to work, we have to provide time and labor. Supplying time and labor means that we are restricted. That is, by the common consciousness fated by "dietary desire consciousness," the life entities on the earth are unconditionally directed to the same ecological activities, called *work*. This is a restriction of a physical body. If we did not have a body we would not have to work.

In order to obtain a chain of life, we must have reproductive activity. In order to preserve the species, we should make a relationship (marriage) and bear children. After giving birth, we have a duty to support our children and to provide time and work for childcare and housework. That is, by the common consciousness fated by "sexual desire consciousness," the life entities on the earth are unconditionally directed to the obligation called reproduction and duty to support children by the same ecological activities.

By these two major desires, human beings made the *requirement and obligation called work and marriage,* mechanized and systematized the social structure based on *the "principle of dependence and domination,"* and have continued to exist unchanged, directed to inconvenience by retention of old-fashioned ideas.

The "instinctive survival consciousnesses" are the common desire consciousnesses fated to all life entities existing on the earth star. Since the origin of bacteria, the primitive life entities, these two "instinctive survival consciousnesses" have changed to various desire consciousnesses through the process of evolution.

2-7. Transitions of "instinctive survival consciousnesses" in history

The "dietary desire consciousness" of human beings has changed to various consciousness forms beginning with a mere securement of energies, and in order to severely survive the process of evolution, it has used various desires as a driving force and achieved evolution by adapting to severe environments. It is no exaggeration to say that human beings have achieved evolution by making the best effort for this desire consciousness in order to reign over the top of the food chain. In present times, human beings have strengthened the evil competition principle for acquisition of the excessive physical world benefits and have made a fierce scramble, building up the economic supremacy doctrine all over the world. Looking back on history, because of this desire consciousness, we have been driven by this urge for acquiring wealth and many other material things, and, tragedies called struggles and wars have been repeated any number of times by leaders and dictators who were dominated by the excessive greed for possessions.

This desire has expanded from individual to family, ethnicity, nation, and world, and still now many nations up holding the economic supremacy doctrine are greedily developing the economic war over the hegemony on a world scale. In addition, in some areas, wars have developed, associated with religious conflicts, over the natural resources and petrochemical energies, and as a result, created slaughters and poverty.

The "instinctive survival consciousnesses" have changed the shapes of various "instinctive remaining consciousnesses" throughout the evolutionary process. From the individual to the world, *dietary desire has changed the shape to material desire,* significantly, and caused fierce, desire centered, evil competition principle to strengthen globally, falling into values directed to the economic supremacy principle, and then made the economic competition scramble even worse.

"Sexual desire consciousness" has changed shape to sexual

Chapter Two ☆ The Deriving Point

drive, for expansion of one's own species and chain of life. More specifically, the "sexual desire consciousness" has been strongly given to male, and significantly become phenomenon as the boss type sexual dominating structure and manifested as the pyramidal type dominating structure. Male exercises a struggle consciousness during a breeding season, and winning with power he displays and maintains the right to acquire many females and the right of domination over the entire group, and has built the pyramid type dominating structure using the boss-type sexual desire domination.

As you can see here, sexual drive has clearly changed shape to the dominating desire, and dominating desire and material desire have created the energy of power, domination, struggle, and destruction. So, as a result, we have built the sad and unfortunate history called struggles and wars. As the saying goes, "Great men have great fondness for the sensual pleasures." Many agree that numerous dictators, politicians, bureaucrats, religious gurus and executives of companies, those who are in a position of domination, have strong sexual and material desires, and history has been built under this fact.

This dominating desire drives people to acquisition competition for others evaluation and that has changed the shape to academic supremacy doctrine and it becomes a center of bureaucracy, building the bureaucratic type dominating structure. The bureaucratic dominating structures in the central governments have built exactly the same structural form with the boss type dominating structure of a monkey society, and they climb aiming for the top of the pyramidal dominating structure according to the evil competition principle called success desire, and as soon as one of them reigns over the top of the victory group, other members disappear from the organization. They have become the incarnation of greed by their dominating desire, and in order to enjoy the vested interests of each other, they have built the "Amakudari organization" (a practice of retired high-ranking bureaucrats taking up executive posts at corporations, and government-affiliated organizations, etc.).

2-8. The terrestrial life has common desire consciousness and performs common ecological action

Since these *"instinctive survival consciousnesses" are the common consciousnesses for all things living on the earth,* all-living things complete the life cycle by common ecological behaviors.

For example, ants travel in paths, one going left and one going right, and will spend their lives repeating the path, back and forth, to secure food for the queen ant and her children in order to preserve the species. Animals also repeat, following their animal trails back and forth from their lair, getting food for their family for preservation of the species, and will continue this pattern until they die. It is the same with human beings. We repeat the pattern of going to work in traffic congestion and trains full of people on the back and forth roads and tracks which are the pathways of humans, and will spend most of our lives repeating, going back and forth, in order to obtain food for our families and preserve the species.

Ants come and go the paths of ants, animals go back and forth on the paths of animals, and humans come and go on the paths of humans. Although ants, animals, and humans are different in morphology and behaviors, the fundamental exercise

Chapter Two ☆ The Deriving Point

of consciousness and direction of motivation are exactly the same, and in accordance with the "instinctive survival consciousnesses," based on the rule that "body is subjective and spirit is objective," all consistently live to complete the "dietary desire consciousness" and "sexual desire consciousness."

The structure of the primitive life entity, bacteria, is composed of clusters of extremely simple molecular structure. It is the relative structure of amino acids which have the molecular structure to complete the "dietary desire consciousness" and create energy for living, and DNA, which has the molecular structure to complete the "sexual desire consciousness" and sustain the chain of life. It is the spiral structure of DNA that has played the role and responsibility of genetic linkage, and this is the evidence of the fact that *all life entities on the earth exist with the same DNA as the common denominator,* from bacteria to viruses, to amoeba, amphibians, reptiles, insects, fish, birds, plants, animals, and human beings.

DNA is composed of the smallest molecular structure, called mononucleotide, in which sugar, nucleic acid, and phosphoric acid are connected as a cluster, and the clusters of molecules of DNA gather and compose the four molecular structures called adenine (A), cytosine(C), guanine (G), thymine (T). Our body has inherited the blueprint of the life circuit called DNA, which was created by those four molecular structures, A, C, G, and T, from our life founder called bacteria, spending the 3.8 billion years throughout ancestry and lineage, according to *the "rule of genetic linkage" based on the "rule of the causality of body."*

Since the "instinctive survival consciousnesses" are the fated consciousnesses for the lives on the earth star, they will continue to remain forever, as long as the body exists, as the fundamental common consciousness for the entire life entities on the earth, no matter how the life entities differentiate to achieve evolution.

By these two major desires, human beings have mechanized *marriage and work,* and systematized the form of male type dominating structure by *the "principle of dependence and domination."* We have continued an unbroken and unchanged existence, directed to inconvenience and domination, for 3.8 billion years.

2-9. Spiritual evolution is the release from "instinctive survival consciousnesses"

All life entities on the earth spend their lifetime with the common ecological behavior which is called predatory action and reproductive action under the common desire consciousness by the "instinctive survival consciousnesses," so other than that, their time is spent resting or sleeping.

Although religions insist that the original sins of human beings are the domination desire based on sexual desire, and the material desire based on dietary desire, they are not accidentally derived because people were depraved. If we define what the original sins are, we could say they are the "original existence consciousnesses," which have been carried as our fate, continuously, from the original life entity, bacteria, since recorded history.

Monkeys, which are said to be close to human beings, dominate the group and command by showing their superiority by the sexual system called mounting. The structural arrangement of Bonobos

Chapter Two ☆ The Deriving Point

(gracile chimpanzee), which are the closest to the human ecosystem, is consistent with human by 99 percent. By observing the ecological behaviors of Bonobos, we can learn about the essential differences between human beings and them. They perform sexual relations regardless of male or female, dozens of times a day as a means of communication in order to keep the power and the balance of the group.

In the social structure of Bonobos, in order to attain the position of the boss, a male need to obtain the trust and confidence of many females by sexual relations. All decisions by the boss are approved and carried out by sexual relations. They vary the behavior of the ecosystem of sexual relations to love expression or domination by sexual desire. The size of the conquered group will be determined by the number and abilities of females which are able to take the sexual relations. By one boss at the top, a pyramidal structure in accordance with the boss type sexual domination is formed and an order to lead the entire group is made.

In human society, throughout history and centered around the royal blood, polygamy has been legalized by the male type sexual desire dominating structure by having a legal wife and many concubines, and carried out the preservation of the species and expansion of territory, and built the pyramidal dominating structure to reign over the country.

Therefore, instead of the sexual corruption of Izanagi and Izanami in the Kojiki (the Legendary stories of old Japan) or, Adam and Eve in the Bible, who were said to be the first human beings, we as human beings have only practiced the ecological behaviors in accordance with the sexual desire consciousness based on the rule of "body is subjective and spirit is objective" by the "instinctive survival consciousnesses."

Corruption means to fall into the lower dimension by departing from the primary position in the spiritual dimension, like falling from the perfect condition into an incomplete one. If there is a definition of corruption in the life entities on the earth, bacteria, as our original life entity, has already fallen to corruption by being burdened with the "instinctive survival consciousnesses" as fate. In that case, we can say that *the "original existence consciousnesses" mean the "original sin consciousnesses."* According to that definition, the life entities on the earth star were born with corruption as their fate. So what would that mean and suggest to us?

2-10. Sexual maturity and spiritual evolution

The level of the spiritual dimension for human beings will be concluded by how you release yourself from the two common major desire consciousnesses, and direct yourself toward spiritual world benefits instead of physical world benefits, and how you differentiated your sexuality to higher human being.

Sexual maturity in the PARAREVO theory is to differentiate the logic of each woman and man to the opposite direction, according to the "rule of entropy relativity" and to achieve evolution to the higher dimension. Based on the "rule of entropy relativity," male and female are connoted the opposite conflicting nature in the consciousness. Male has acquired *the logic of power, domination, struggle, and destruction* in his consciousness, and female has acquired *the logic of love, integration, harmony, and creation* in her consciousness.

Chapter Two ☆ The Deriving Point

So, according to the "principle of dimensional integration," when a woman with the relative subjectivity keeps increasing and strengthening the logic of love, integration, harmony, and creation, and a man with the relative objectivity keeps decreasing and weakening the logic of power, domination, struggle, and destruction, it will make the possibility to develop sexual maturity and achieve spiritual evolution.

The strength and weakness of the physical desire consciousness varies in the degree of the "instinctive remaining consciousnesses" through the process of spiritual evolution. That is to say, it is determined by whether the "instinctive survival consciousnesses" remain strongly, according to the rule of "body is subjective and spirit is objective," or whether Self-Enlightenment and spiritual evolution are done releasing the physical desire and domination according to the rule of "spirit is subjective and body is objective." The strength of sexual desire and material desire, and the level of the personality and spirituality in the spiritual dimension, are also determined by that.

The "sexual desire consciousness" and the "dietary desire consciousness" have been strengthened through evolution as our "instinctive remaining consciousnesses," and the former has changed to the status desire and reputation desire, and the latter has changed to the material desire, but still both remain as the core of the desires no matter the evolution progress.

When a person has a strong desire and persistence for status, honor, and material possessions, the person's spiritual evolution is slower. This proves that he is in the lower spiritual dimension which is the same level as Bonobos. The crucial difference between human beings as highly dimensional Homo sapiens and anthropoid ape, such as orangutans, gorillas and chimpanzees, is determined by whether they have *an undifferentiated sexual impulse* and constantly desire sexual relations like Bonobos, or they are able to manage their sexual desires by connoting *"high-dimensional sexual orders."*

The difference between ordinal animals and anthropoid apes is that anthropoid apes have frequent sexual relations regardless of the breeding season or weather the partner is male or female. A person who has sexual desire with sexual immaturity in the consciousness has a tendency to look for particular sex and love in homosexual and heterosexual relationships.

By evolving sexual maturity of woman and man to a higher dimension, and channeling their sexual desire to true love, it will be possible to achieve Self-Enlightenment and spiritual evolution to a higher spiritual dimension as a new higher dimensional human race.

2-11. Release of undifferentiated sexual desire consciousness and spiritual evolution

Human beings have endlessly strengthened both the physical desire and the spiritual desire heading for the top of the food chain, and built the culture and the civilization together. Human beings have released the "instinctive survival consciousnesses" and constructed the spiritual evolution and the mental culture throughout history. At the same time, by the "rule of entropy relativity" (to see 2-39 for more detail), we have developed the

Chapter Two ☆ The Deriving Point

material civilization by the progress of science. However, it also means this has invited the global crisis of human annihilation by the development of the nuclear bomb as a mass destruction weapon.

Thus, based on the "rule of entropy relativity," something which has a counter nature, such as physical desire and spiritual desire, exists simultaneously and synchronically. The spiritual desire is the relative subjectivity and the physical desire is the relative objectivity. So, the strengthening of the spiritual desire promotes a development of the mental culture, and the strengthening of the physical desire promotes development of the material civilization. However, when one is strengthened and developed, the other is also developed at the same time, so it never happens that only one thing is developed and the other stays the same. The mental culture and the material civilization have strengthened together in the process of evolution.

The problem of the physical desire, the relative objectivity, is that it held a dominant position, and only developed the material civilization, but the opposite, the mental culture, has held little importance. We can prove this with the fact that we are living in an environment far developed from the material civilization of 2,000 years ago, but the mental culture has hardly evolved, limited by the heritage of religious scriptures and doctrines. If the relative subjectivity has held a dominant position, and the degree of strengthening of the mental culture has exceeded, human beings would never have foolishly thought to develop the nuclear bomb to control civilization.

By this theory, between men and women the relative subjectivity is women and the relative objectivity is men. Therefore, women have a very important role in the development of the mental culture. The delay in the mental culture means the delay in the role of women on the earth star.

Depending on the surviving strength of the "instinctive remaining consciousnesses," the criterion of the soul as the spirituality of the person and the criterion of the mind as the personality dimension will manifest as the spiritual dimension.

For example, a person who has a strong material desire, which has been derived from the dietary desire, will have an extremely slow spiritual evolution, because he has a materialistic personality being dominated by the economic supremacy principle. Also, a person who has a strong desire for status and honor, which has been derived from sexual desire, is severely underdeveloped in his sexual maturity and is dominant toward women. This is typical of a person with the male type dominating structure who has a strong and violent disrespect for women, connoting undifferentiated sexual desire consciousness.

The issue of the undifferentiated sexual desire consciousness is the problem of a complex cluster of personality and spirituality that has accumulated throughout history. It is not a question of high or low intelligence, but is the essential issue in the spiritual dimension of the spiritual consciousness entity itself.

Those in a managerial position or officers, who have social standing and honors, would not reach that dominating class without this desire. They always keep the sexual impulse by undifferentiated sexual desire in the consciousness and live a life with extremely tenuous *cultural contributions to sexuality,* which means that men support women humbly and seriously, and build

Chapter Two ☆ The Deriving Point

the ideal love world.

In fact, men who have strong sexual domination desires and are infatuated with women tend to have a high success rate in life because poor personality of undifferentiated sexual desire and personality with strong material desire are synchronized. It is not an overstatement to say that the path to Self-Enlightenment and spiritual evolution for human beings has been closed because only those persons who have the both personalities have gone up to the top of the pyramidal dominating structure.

For example, the arrogant bureaucrats, politicians, cult gurus, and bad corporate executives have *the sexual disabilities that keep undifferentiated sexual desire inside* and they are the ones most likely to conduct sexual harassment or power harassment openly. Since those who are underdeveloped in sexual maturity are often missing their maternal love, they are extremely strong in dominating desire consciousness over women, and many of them succeed to a dominating position in this world, like Bonobos.

It is no exaggeration to say that the evolution of the life entities on the earth is *the cultural history of sexual maturity*.form of "sex separation life entity" that was sexually distinct, into female and male, evolving from anthropoid ape to Homo erectus (two legged people), to Homo habilis (people who use tools) and to Homo sapiens (people who have knowledge). Homo sapiens in the lower spiritual dimension are dominated by *"undifferentiated sexual desire consciousness,"* like Bonobos, and always contain the sexual impulse for the opposite sex, inside the consciousness. Since Homo philosophical (philosophical people) in the higher spiritual dimension have established *"high-level differentiated sexual ethics,"* they form sexual order with Self-management not only toward sexual impulse to the same sex but also of sexual desire toward the opposite sex.

2-12. Subconscious is derived from the physical and spiritual formation history

All consciousnesses of the life entities on the earth star have started from the "instinctive survival consciousnesses" that were fated at the moment the soul, the spiritual consciousness entity, carried the body. So the evolution of the spiritual consciousness entity and the physical body, have been directed by the following rule.

The evolution of the spiritual consciousness entity has been achieved, according to the "rule of spiritual causality" based on the rule of "spirit is subjective and body is objective," and repeated the descent from the spiritual world to this world, over and over again, by reincarnation.

The human body has achieved physical evolution, according to the "rule of physical causality" based on the rule of "body is subjective and spirit is objective," and repeated the genetic modification by genetic linkage.

The "instinctive survival consciousnesses" have formed the

cluster of the soul, accumulating consciousness to evolution slowly, complying with the role and responsibility according to the rule of "spirit is subjective and body is objective," adhering to the genetic codes, and strengthening each spirituality formation history along with physical formation history. This has formed the cluster of the complex consciousnesses by completing the evolutional process for the spirit and the body in each age. These are collectively called *subconscious*.

The formation process of the subconscious is derived from the spiritual and the physical formation history, based on environments and experiences. The spirituality formation history, called the direct subconscious, is also called *"reincarnation consciousness,"* because this consciousness is the aggregation of consciousnesses being formed by the "rule of reincarnation" from past lives to the one just previous to our present life.

The physical formation history, called the indirect subconscious, is also called the *"genetic consciousness,"* because it is the aggregation of genetic information in the physical evolution process and is based on the genetic code.

2-13. "Reincarnation consciousness" is the direct subconscious

The spirituality formation history of our soul is an aggregated memory of the soul based on our own direct experiences, repeating many times in this world, according to the "rule of reincarnation," and occupies the biggest part of our consciousnesses, as potential consciousness.

The subconscious exists as the cluster of the spiritual consciousness entity, which is built continuously in the environments of each era and historical background through our direct experiences, according to the "rule of reincarnation." This formation is based on the "rule of spiritual causality" by the rule of "spirit is subjective and body is objective." Since these are the direct experiences of our soul, this aggregation of consciousnesses is called the direct subconscious, or "reincarnation consciousness."

How does the memory of this direct subconscious influence our life? The way a person lived, whether he had been contributing to people and society, and living a life admired by many people, with *the memory of the soul* up to the previous past life that has aggregated the spirituality formation history to goodness based on love, having a mind of benevolence in the past life, or whether he lived causing distress and hardship to many people and been disliked by people and society, with *the memory of the soul* that has aggregated the poor spirituality formation history to the evil, based on ONSHU, deceiving the public with a malicious mind. There are obviously big differences in the exercising of the consciousness toward the purpose and values in this world, and speech and behavior based on motivation, and size and weight of tests toward assignment responsibility.

2-14. "Genetic consciousness" is the indirect subconscious

The most familiar physical consciousness traits in the physical formation history are in the genetic information inherited from

Chapter Two ☆ The Deriving Point

parents. The parents, of course, also inherited the genetic information from the grandparents who inherited it from their parents, etc. Thus, according to the genetic linkage by the "rule of physical causality" of parents and child, inherited genetic information over 3.8 billion years through blood lineage are aggregated into each of the 60 trillion cells in the body and create the cluster of the body.

According to the eternal genetic linkage of the body, kinship of the parents and child has never ceased, but continuously inherited genes and exist in this world by the fact of the physical formation history. This aggregation of the physical consciousness is called the indirect subconscious or the "genetic consciousness," because it has not been built through our direct experiences, but is the memory of DNA inherited from our ancestors through the lineage.

This subconscious has recombined the genetic information of the physical evolution to the genetic structural arrangement each time, and filled it in as a new memory of the genetic code according to the genetic chain based on physical causality by the rule of "body is subjective and spirit is objective," throughout the lineage. This indirect subconscious has nothing to do with the formation process of the soul, but is only connected with the physical body, so the formation process in the soul and the body is clearly different.

How does the indirect subconscious influence our life? It makes quite a difference in the spiritual dimension and the concept for existing purpose and values to live in this world. Whether, for example, it is the lineage enslaved by the physical desire according to the rule of "body is subjective and spirit is objective," and dominated by the sexual desire and the desire for such things as status, honor and material possessions for excessive physical world benefits and had lived the greedy and momentary life, or whether it is the lineage, according to the spiritual theoretical framework and values, releasing the soul from the instinctive desire domination by overcoming the genetic consciousness and the physical domination, by love.

So, if our DNA consciousness inherited the strong instinctive desire consciousness, it will manifest as uncontrollable desires for things such as status, honor, or material possessions and would appear as an obvious phenomenon in habits and illnesses such as twisted nature, thievish habits, cancers, incurable diseases and/or strange diseases.

Many religions persuade with the theory of punitive justice, fate, and luck. However, those are talking about the indirect subconscious in the physical level that has been inherited by the genetic chain through the lineage based on physical causality by the rule of "body is subjective and spirit is objective," and there is no direct causal relationship with the soul, our spiritual consciousness entity.

2-15. The fundamental difference between subconscious of the soul and the body

Subconscious is a deep consciousness that we are not able to see, as though it were an iceberg submerged below sea level. The "consciousness of reincarnation," the direct subconscious, is also called "past life consciousness aggregation entity," because in the spiritual world, the soul itself has determined its own mother's fertilized egg which became the body on the earth and challenged the spiritual evolution, according to the rule of "spirit is subjective and body is objective." It then descended to this world by the "rule of reincarnation," and formed the cluster of the spiritual consciousness entity by directing the memory of the soul to a higher level with its own direct experiences and rewriting it to new memory of the soul, according to the *"rule of preservation by inscription,"* and repeating its own spiritual evolution.

The direct subconscious forms the pillars of the spirituality together with the history, and it forms the backbone of the soul, as if in our physical body, with brain and spinal cord as its central nervous system.

The "genetic consciousness," the indirect subconscious, is the information aggregation entity of DNA, which has been continuously inherited by the lineage throughout the evolutional history of 3.8 billion years through parents and ancestors. This subconscious is also called the "genetic consciousness aggregation entity."

It is my conclusion that *the direct subconscious is the past life consciousness derived from the "rule of reincarnation" based on the rule that "spirit is subjective and body is objective," and has played a role and responsibility in the spiritual evolution. The indirect subconscious, the "genetic consciousness," is derived from the genetic chain based on the rule of "body is subjective and spirit is objective" and has played a role and responsibility in the physical evolution.* This complex entity spiritually forms mental disposition and physically forms physical predisposition.

2-16. Law of causality in Buddhism theory is untruth

The rules of "retributive justice" and "luck and fate" are the central doctrine of Buddhism, which has been openly and plausibly inherited, without any doubt, as truth in the history of Buddhism. These rules are considered the most important theories in Buddhism and have created the concept of ancestral memorial services on the line of extended idea. These ideas are the hotbed of the physical world benefits in existing and rising Buddhism related religion groups.

The ancestral memorial service based on these ideas is directed this way.

> Your happiness right now is in virtue of your parents who gave you a life in this world, and it ascends to your ancestors, so you should express your gratitude to them also. Because of your ancestors, all your blood relations are created in this world and as a result it created all your happiness or unhappiness. Thus, your ancestors are like the origin of the stream, they are upstream, and you are standing downstream to receive the flow. So, if you are not happy now it is not you but your ancestors fault. They are sending you the flow of unhappiness. You are just receiving it.

It continues to guide you in the direction of shifting responsibility by making you slip into victim mentality by making your ancestors out as criminal or evil with untruth theory.

Ultimately, it says that *if you do not hold memorial services for ancestors, more tragic accidents would happen to your children and family as bad Karma.* It binds people up with a rope called fear and anxiety, trying to make them plunge into mental disabilities, and brainwash them by directing to *the "principle of dependency and domination"* which cult groups are good at. These untrue and fake logics are used for starting new religions and to get members in new cult groups.

Chapter Two ☆ The Deriving Point

The PARAREVO theory clearly distinguishes the theoretical framework and value between the "rule of reincarnation" based on "spirit is subjective and body is objective," and the "rule of genetic linkage" based on "body is subjective and spirit is objective." Those two direct to the totally opposite way with the paradoxical theory, and strictly suggest the paradigm regarding the subjective and cause or the objective and effect.

Thus, we achieve spiritual evolution, according to the intention which is directed by the love of the spiritual consciousness entity, the "soul mind." On the other hand, the physical desire, the "body mind," directs the spiritual degeneration. The two are just like an accelerator and a brake, and directed by the opposite nature based on the "rule of entropy relativity." However, with the "soul mind," the relative subjective, we are certainly achieving evolution by defeating the desire of the "body mind," the relative objective.

How many ancestors do you think exist through the 30 generations when we trace our physical ancestors from parents to grandparents, great-grandparents and more? Even just going back 30 generations, counting backward, there are about 11 million ancestors and as the integral value, it goes much over 16 billion ancestors, and if even one person had missed this family tree, you would not exist in this world. Let's suppose that one generation is 20 years, 30 generations ago is only 600 years ago, and we already have quite numbers of ancestors. However, our life chain is not only 600 years. If we seek to visit former ancestors and trace back to the terminus point of the trip of the far and eternal life chain, how many ancestors do we have? Probably, it should be cosmological numbers of ancestors. And it is sure that when we go back to the starting point after seeing and visiting the ancestors of 3.8 billion years, we will reach the original life entity, bacteria. Bacteria are the real ancestor of all life in and on the earth, and we have continued the trip of the life chain for 3.8 billion years continuously without cutting off the chain.

Since DNA exists to play the role and responsibility as a guide for the physical evolution and preserve the species as the leading part for the genetic chain, all life in and on the earth, from bacteria to human beings, has evolved with DNA as the common guide. We have inherited DNA, which is the blueprint of the life circuit, from our ancestors, but never inherited the soul itself. The process of physical evolution has unbrokenly continued up to the present by the "rule of physical causality" as parents and children, according to the memory of DNA based on the rule of "body is subjective and spirit is objective." In the 60 trillion cells of our body, we have continuously inherited the structural arrangement of the genetic DNA from our ancestors, inevitably, and it exists as an undeniable fact in us.

If we describe a memorial service for ancestors, the most appropriate way will be taking care of ourselves. That is *the true memorial service for ancestors*. Because you are the product of 3.8 billion years of ancestors, which has been inherited and created in your own genes. Memorial service is written as *people maintain each other,* in Japanese. Thus, you should take care of your own body with deep gratitude as a precious irreplaceable thing because it has continuously inherited the history of the physical evolution in an astounding amount of time and it exists as undeniable fact in the present as bearing the treasure of 3.8 billion years. Therefore, *taking care of the body that coexists with the soul is the real memorial service for ancestors,* so there is no connection between ancestors and your soul at all.

The rule of the universe is that *sins made by ancestors should be completed by ancestors based on the "rule of reincarnation" according to the Self-responsibility principle of ancestors.* This is the principle of Self-determination, Self-responsibility and Self-completion, based on the "rule of freedom" by the PARAREVO theory, so freedom should be completed together with responsibility.

It starts with the funeral, then Buddhist memorial services such as the first seven days, forty-nine days, the first death anniversary, third year, seventh year, and thirteenth year anniversaries are considered as holding memorial services to the spirit, however, those services are actually held for the ones who were left in this world, for releasing their debt to the deceased, and for Self-satisfaction and comfort. It is often times only a ceremony for appearances and vanity, and these memorial services and masses are all conducts that those who live in this world hold but have nothing to do with those who passed away to the spiritual world. Since the Buddhist ideology of commemoration of ancestors is collapsed by the PARAREVO theory, I strongly suggest that Buddhist monks should withdraw from falsehood and fake ceremonies and Buddhist services and stay away from the physical world benefits, promptly.

2-17. Genetic linkage and reincarnation are both related to the principle of Self-responsibility

According to the PARAREVO theory, the "cosmological evidence" is this. *Everything is based on the "rule of freedom," so you have done everything by your own determination, and you should take Self-responsibility for the phenomenon which happened because of your deeds, and direct to Self-completion.*

People who live the PARAREVO way direct themselves to the Self-Enlightenment and spiritual evolution by Self-responsibility and attain real freedom by bearing the responsibility of real independence without blaming or depending on something or someone else.

Ancestors never depend on descendants for help. Those who have gone to the spiritual world have already decided which spiritual dimension they would go to, according to the way of life they had in this world, so we should leave it to their own Self-responsibility.

Even if someone can raise a heavy soul from the lower-dimension to higher position by the seemingly irresponsible idea of Messiah or ideology of salvation by relying upon others, that soul will fall back down to the original lower position when the efforts of others weaken. If you want to stay in a higher position forever, in the spiritual world, you have to make your soul light by your own effort. This is the basic idea of the PARAREVO theory.

If, as Buddhism says, the souls of ancestors are saved by holding memorial services for them, the principle of Self-responsibility would collapse and the fundamental system of the principle of freedom in the universe would be destroyed and the result would be the extinction of the universe itself. Also, there is another service called memorial services for your past life. If that system works, the "rule of reincarnation" itself would be completely reversed and there would be no reason to be born to this world again. If you truly understand the system of the spiritual world, you would never bring things from the afterlife into this world, or attempt to intervene with such things as memorial services.

The "principle of reincarnation" is the rule of Self-determination and Self-responsibility, and is also the fundamental principle based on the cosmological evidence, which is to carry out your own salvation by yourself. In other words, you are the only one who can make amends for your past sins, and if you do not do it now, you will eventually have to, perhaps even in a future life.

Even though the direct subconscious holds the greatest portion of the core of our spirituality, and the indirect subconscious is only the dominating structure of DNA, which is only the surface of the physical consciousness, most people are dominated by the physical desires and live their lives worldly, materialistically and momentary.

2-18. Emerging consciousnesses are formed in two stages

The formation processes of the emerging consciousnesses are derived from the personality formation history. The personality formation history is divided into two stages by two totally different environments and experiences.

The first stage comes from the personality formation history based on the environment and experience in the 40 weeks of prenatal life.

The second stage comes from the personality formation history based on the environment and experience in life on the earth after birth.

2-19. The purpose of the personality formation and the physical body formation in the prenatal life

The beginning of the personality formation history starts when tens of millions of sperm swim toward the egg and at the moment an egg accepts a sperm, the egg emits a living light by receiving the spiritual consciousness entity, the soul. The fertilized egg is then implanted on the uterine wall and the placenta is formed uniting a mother and a child, then a prenatal life of 40 weeks begins.

The purpose of the prenatal life is nothing more than a preparation period for a good earth life after birth. We do not need hands, feet, mouth, and nose in the womb, but all are necessary after birth for living in the earth star.

The environment and experience in the prenatal life forms the core of the personality and the body. It is the important preparation period, and will even direct fate itself, on the earth life.

2-20. Ideal personality formation in the prenatal life

To make an ideal personality formation for a fetus, it is important and essential for a husband and wife to form a mutual assistance program between them for the good of the fetus. Also, in order to make personality formation for a higher spiritual dimension, it is important for the couple to treat each other tenderly, love each other, understand each other and foster each other with love, and it is especially essential to create a prenatal environment which is dimensionally integrated in maternal love, and also important for them to aim for a dimensionally higher life, with their hearts full of

Chapter Two ☆ The Deriving Point

love, preparing the life environment for the personality formation for the fetus, and spending every day with gratitude and happiness.

By her own efforts, a mother should practice spiritually stable love to her fetus, and make her womb the best prenatal environment with love and peace, and allow her fetus to experience the bonds of love between a mother and her child. Even though a husband won't be able to unite directly with his child, he should make efforts of paternal love with all his heart, and give the paternal love to his child indirectly through his wife's mind and soul by loving and treating his wife tenderly.

People who live the way of PARAREVO establish their view of life as the collective, by fostering maternal love together with the fetus, toward a higher dimension. And based on the "rule of change by birth and rebirth," the mother's own spiritual consciousness entity will be rebirthed to a higher dimension by the re-birth of the mind and spirit of the fetus to a higher dimension.

The "rule of change by birth and rebirth" is to achieve Self-Enlightenment and spiritual evolution by carrying out the spiritual quality improvement (the mental disposition) and the physical improvement (the physical predisposition) of the fetus in the womb. Thus, it is the rule that the mother herself will be re-birthed by changing the soul and the body of the fetus (See 2-24 and 2-26 for more details).

The best way for a woman to achieve spiritual evolution is to switch her consciousness from obscene sexual relations to sacred sexual conception based on spiritual intelligence and spiritual sense, and to conceive a fetus with a sacred soul. The chance for a woman to attain physical evolution is to improve the physical predisposition of her fetus with her consciousness to accept the sperm of a man, by sacred sexual conception based on spiritual intelligence and spiritual sense, according to the rule of "soul is subjective and body is objective."

This is because the mother is the one to exist as the actual result for the manifestation of the fetus's spirituality formation history from the past to the previous past life. Therefore, when the mother raises her personality formation to a higher dimension during her pregnancy, the spiritual quality improvement of the fetus is accomplished based on the environment and the experiences in the womb, and the mind and spirit of the fetus will be improved according to the "rule of preservation by inscription." The mother should spend her pregnancy period carefully examining her own time as a fetus in her mother's womb, and making the changes she feels necessary for the good of her own fetus.

2-21. Taboos of personality formation in the womb

We should be aware that the 40 weeks of prenatal life are the important preparation period to form the backbone and framework of a child, which is the core of the personality formation and the physical formation for the earth life.

Based on the PARAREVO theory, the fetus that spends it prenatal life with love and compassion from the parents will form the core of love, which is the most necessary for personality, and the core of DNA, which is the most necessary for the body. So, after they are born in this world they can live a mentally and physically stable life.

On the other hand, if the fetus had a poor prenatal life, such as with a young couple who did not receive love from their parents, could not be independent, became pregnant without knowing what society really was, constantly quarrelling, abusing and blaming each other with negative feelings and feuding with their in-laws, the fetus was basically poisoned by its own mother and was constantly intimidated by its father's violence, which caused personality destruction and mental anguish by feeling every aspect of the mother's negative and immature feelings.

Self-injurious behavior by the mother's Self-hatred and Self-denial seriously hurt the mind and spirit of the fetus. As a result of this, the child becomes withdrawn, depressed, and delinquent, refusing go to school, bullying, and becomes the typical example of "NEET" (no employment, education or training) with constant negative feelings. In the end, he/she often creates a bad environment by and for him/herself and ultimately falls into committing violent crimes such as abusing or killing his/her own children.

2-22. Ideal physical formation in the prenatal life

Physically, a mother has to learn a breathing method which will supply enough oxygen, and aim for a good balanced life, absorbing plenty of energy waves from the sun and moon. Of course, she should take in enough nutrition such as minerals and vitamins, which are necessary for the fetus, and to avoid the amniotic fluid becoming turbid. She should also avoid unnecessary physical exertion which could put physical stress on the fetus, and avoid anything else which may have negative influence on the fetus.

It is especially important to improve the mother's lifestyle by things such as no smoking or drinking of alcohol, and prevent the blood from contamination by controlling the outbreak of active oxygen and arresting DNA destruction and cell destruction. Also, it is important to increase immunity from disease by removing active oxygen and eating healthy foods including lots of green vegetables, which will rapidly purify the blood. It is also essential to do moderate exercise.

2-23. Taboos of physical formation in the prenatal life

It is taboo for a pregnant woman to drink alcohol or use any drugs such as stimulants, smoking, and/or excessive intake of food additives and preservatives such as in processed and premade foods. The excessive intake of animal fat and protein should also be avoided. As an extreme example, the fetus will be at great risk if a pregnant mother who takes stimulants and drugs because of the stress of pregnancy, eats too much, is addicted to tobacco and/or alcohol, or becomes dependent on hard drugs, will be Self-poisoning her own womb.

I have cited these two contrasting examples in 2-22 and this 2-23 to show how the formation of the personality and the body in the prenatal life will determine more than 90 percent of child's life style on the earth.

All things have meaning. The purpose of the prenatal life is only for the preparation period for the earth life. It is nothing more or less than that.

Chapter Two ☆ The Deriving Point

2-24. Womb is a sanctuary for "change by birth and re-birth"

Parents, in general, tend to think that they start to raise their child after birth, however, that is too late to start. While the fetus is in the womb, the mother can raise her child in any way she wishes, however, from the moment of birth, the child is already an individual life entity with a separate character, so it is extremely difficult to raise her child as she wants.

The prenatal life is an important period for the fetus and the mother, because they are united by a single umbilical cord. It is also a mysterious period because two totally different life entities co-exist. During this period, the spiritual consciousness entity and the body of mother and fetus sympathize with each other in the joint ownership of the feelings of maternal love and the life of the irreplaceable and precious fetus. The fetus then achieves the personality formation of ideal love and strong physical formation, together, which becomes the core of the spiritual consciousness entity through the interchange of love, to accomplish the spiritual and the physical evolution.

Of course, at this time, a lot of maternal love also grows in the mother, with the child in her womb, and the spiritual evolution and the physical purification for both mother and child create the ideal personality of love simultaneously by *the "rule of change by birth and re-birth."* Since the spiritual evolution by the real improvement of spiritual quality will be completed when a mother and child are united by impregnation, this will be the most important period in the history of evolution.

The soul of a child, the spiritual consciousness entity, selects a fertilized egg which becomes father and mother for the fetus and appears as pregnancy, according to the "rule of reincarnation" based on the rule of "soul is subjective and body is objective," according to Self-determination based on the "rule of freedom." Since parents can't choose their children, their wish would never be fulfilled even if they wish to bear excellent, great and ideal ones. Of course, it is not even possible to choose a boy or girl.

Thus, *the soul of the spiritual consciousness entity of the child is the cause and the subject of the right to choose the fertilized egg of the parents, and the genes of the parents are the result and the object being selected as a body.* At the same time, the body of the fetus inherits the DNA of 3.8 billion years of ancestors from the sperm and egg of parents, and is born in this world, according to the genetic linkage based on the rule of "body is subjective and soul is objective."

2-25. Womb is a sanctuary for physical evolution

What kind of mechanism made the differentiation and achieved evolution from bacteria to various kinds of life entities on the earth? The PARAREVO theory clearly verifies and explains this evolution mechanism, cosmologically.

According to the mechanism for physical evolution, when the mother's body is contaminated by toxins such as dioxin, cadmium, or mercury, and becomes ill, it is nearly impossible to excrete the contaminants from the body by modern medical science. However, there is only one way to cleanse the body of contaminants and excrete them. That is to become pregnant. By being pregnant, a placenta is formed and through it the fetus grows by absorbing

Chapter Two ☆ The Deriving Point

oxygen and nutrients from the mother's body.

The placenta is an important transit point to connect between the fetus and the mother's body, so it is no exaggeration to say that the placenta is the third life entity. The placenta purifies the body toxins and contaminants inside the mother's body to prevent them from reaching the fetus, and plays a role and responsibility as a filter that only provides pure oxygen and rich nutrients. It is a vital organ that can be called the third heart.

When a woman is pregnant, the internal contaminants in her body are absorbed in the placenta. This improves the physical condition for both mother and the fetus, and the contaminants are excreted from the body together with the placenta at the time of birth.

The PARAREVO theory suggests that the ultimate improvement of the physical condition of the universe and the equation for physical evolution are inserted in the mysterious work of the two life entities called pregnancy.

Why does the physical evolution occur? It is because *the "rule of the universe" is that evolution is directed toward a higher individual entity by the "principle of dimensional integration" based on free intention and love.*

When does the physical evolution happen? The guide for physical evolution is genetic DNA. The physical evolution begins the moment an ovum is fertilized by a sperm, and like a single-celled organism such as bacteria and virus, cell division began with a single cell and repeated differentiation along with the memory circuit of DNA throughout the history of evolution in 3.8 billion years, and would reach to the genetic information of the mother and father in less than two months. When new genetic information is inserted as plus alpha, one in the last row of the structural arrangement of the genetic DNA by the intention of the fetus, and achieved the conversion arrangement of the structural order according to the "rule of preservation by inscription," then the physical evolution would be completed as the fetus body after the genetic rearrangement.

Where does the physical evolution happen? The real mechanism of physical evolution, the memory of DNA as the blueprint of the life circuit, is written only in the gene of the mitochondria of women based on the data of environmental adaption on the earth life, and the genetic structural conversion is all done in the uterus.

Who does the physical evolution? According to the rule of "spirit is subjective and body is objective," the relative original power of the personality and intention of mother and fetus, directs the evolution. Up to the time of when the father's sperm fertilizes the mother's ovum, all genetic information for the fetus is old information, so the fetus will be rewriting the genetic information, as the relative body, by the intention and the personality of the spiritual consciousness entity of the fetus, and will accomplish physical evolution by the "rule of preservation by inscription," and be born in this world. This is why siblings born to the same parents are all different in looks and personality.

Physical evolution is definitely not done by the recombination of DNA, mechanically, by merely the adaption to the natural environment and the social environment of earth life. If all life achieves the physical evolution equally, in the same environment, there should not be such a wide variety of life entities on the earth.

The genetic DNA is the common denominator for all life entities

Chapter Two ☆ The Deriving Point

on the earth, so, what is the difference between birds and human beings? It is the difference of the numerator mounted on the common denominator which effect the evolution by *the intention based on the personality*. Birds had the strong individuality and intention to fly, therefore they achieved the evolution to birds based on the rule of "spirit is subjective and body is objective."

Even if someone wishes to be a baseball player, a football player, or professional golfer, not everyone can achieve that easily unless he/she has the natural talent. The natural talent is the power of the will which selects parents by the Self-determination of the intention based on the individuality in the spiritual world directing for Self-realization in this world, based on the rule of "spirit is subjective and body is objective." People who become great artists and scientists have the natural talent because they were born with the strong power of will based on strong intention and individuality, making it possible for them to bring forth outstanding talents in this world.

Even if a mother dreams of her fetus becoming her ideal and wishes only with her intention and individuality, the natural talent is directed by the cause and subjectivity to the intention and individuality of the fetus, so the role and responsibility of the mother is only to support the physical evolution of the fetus by preparing a better environment in the womb. When mother and fetus have matched intention and individuality, the ideal child, like a masterpiece, which has achieved the physical evolution with the natural talent, will be born to this world.

What does the physical evolution do? It makes the improvement of the physical condition by recombination of the gene. The best time and method for the improvement of the physical condition is during the morning sickness period which causes nausea, vomiting and discomfort for the mother in the first 2 to 3 months of pregnancy. One of the reasons for morning sickness may be that the fetus has an unhealthy physical condition or some disorders. Another reason may be that both mother and the fetus have negative feelings relatively. How to improve such a physical condition is in the mother' attitude. She should *accept the morning sickness symptoms unconditionally with gratitude and happiness* based on the rule of "spirit is subjective and body is objective," by changing her mind and spirit from negative feelings to positive feelings.

The intention and individuality of the mother directs the intention and individuality of the fetus to a higher level according to the "rule of dimensional integration," then the improvement of the fetus' physical condition will become possible by the intention of the fetus, and new genes will be inserted and achieve the arrangement conversion in the structural order of the genetic DNA, and recombinant DNA will be completed to the higher level and the physical condition will be improved. The mother will be able to upgrade and complete her own physical condition by achieving the improvement of the physical condition for the fetus and by the mechanism of the mutual aids, *the "rule of change by birth and re-birth,"* based on the PARAREVO theory. If she fails to direct the intention and individuality of the fetus to a higher level, it could result in the possibility of her bearing a child with unhealthy physical conditions or disabilities such as self-immune disease like atopy, asthma, or pollinosis, cancer predisposition, frail constitution or incurable disease predisposition.

How is the physical evolution achieved? The physical evolution is achieved by completing *the "rule of change by birth and re-birth"* of the genetic information through *intrauterine collaboration* of the life entity, which co-exists with mutual prosperity, symbiosis, co-promotion by mutual aids of both mother and child, and directs the primary purpose of the spiritual evolution. When the fetus is integrated in maternal love, by its own intention and individuality, it will be able to achieve the genetic rearrangement and the improvement of the physical condition.

2-26. Womb is a sanctuary for spiritual evolution

The "rule of the universe" is carried by the rule of "spirit is subjective and body is objective," and the "rule of the earth" is carried by the rule of "body is subjective and spirit is objective."

It is suggested by the PARAREVO theory that the mysterious works of life like pregnancy and prenatal life are set in the equation for the ultimate evolution of the universe. The spiritual evolution is nothing but how we omit or reduce the "instinctive survival consciousnesses," which are dietary desire consciousness (material desire) and sexual desire consciousness (status desire and honor desire).

The PARAREVO theory also suggests that the process of evolution starts from the moment of spiritual conception. Spiritual conception is when a woman conceives a fetus by wising to conceive a fetus with a sacred soul based on her spiritual intelligence and spiritual sense, rather than sexual desire. Since evolution is completed in each period by *the "rule of change by birth and re-birth,"* what kind of spiritual consciousness entity from the spiritual world is received by the fertilized egg, becomes an important concept. So, since the *conception descent* of the spiritual consciousness entity of the fetus will be completed by *the "rule of relative original power" based on the mind and spirit in the spiritual dimension,* the spiritual consciousness entity in the spiritual dimension, which is relative to the mother's personality dimension, will descend to her fertilized ovum. Everything is based on the relativity, and at this moment, the phenomenon called the *conception descent* is completed, according to the "rule of relative original power." Because of the fundamental rule of the universe, *the entire universe is the source of power which makes possible the continuing existence of the universe itself, being relative by the relative universal original power.*

Like water and oil repel each other, the spiritual consciousness entity of a higher spiritual dimension will never descend to a mother in a lower personality dimension, which is ignoring the relativity, and the spiritual consciousness entity of a lower spiritual dimension will never descend to a mother in a higher personality dimension. The *conception descent* will be completed based on the relativity of the spiritual dimension. Since there are many different levels in the spiritual dimension, such as the "Astral spiritual decibel dimension," the "Mental spiritual decibel dimension," and the "Causal spiritual decibel dimension," depending on the mother's level, she will receive her fetus from the same level in the spiritual dimension by spiritual conception. Thus, the spiritual evolution already has important meaning and significance from the spiritual conception.

The dimension of mind and spirit of a mother and the spiritual dimension of a fetus are relatively completed. There will be a huge difference between a fetus whose mother became pregnant by a lewd and unloving sexual relationship, only seeking physical pleasures dominated by undifferentiated sexual desire consciousness, and a fetus whose mother became pregnant by intention and with the individuality to wish to receive a pure and sublime spiritual consciousness entity to her womb. Thus, it is no exaggeration to say that *the spiritual evolution is left with the dimension of mind and spirit of mother.*

Since the "rule of freedom" is guaranteed based on intention of the universe, a phenomenon of coincidence does not exist in the universe. The prenatal life is the mysterious period when the fetus and the mother, two totally different life entities, are connected by a single umbilical cord, and co-exist. So their spiritual consciousness and body are sympathizing, and through the exchange of love, they accomplish both an ideal love personality formation and a sturdy physical formation which becomes the core of the spiritual consciousness entity. During this important prenatal life, the fetus and the mother will achieve both the spiritual evolution and the physical evolution by the "rule of change by birth and re-birth."

Based on the relative wave in the spiritual dimension and the "rule of relative original power," the spiritual consciousness entity of the fetus selects the fertilized ovum which contains the genes that provide the role and responsibility which is the assignment for the "instinctive survival consciousnesses" in this world by Self-determination, based on the "rule of freedom," and descends as the spiritual conception according to the "rule of reincarnation." Therefore, the fetus selects the mother who has the same assignment in this world and the same issues in her spirit. The reason is for the spiritual evolution only. However, if the mother is ignorant of the spiritual evolution, she only cares about the healthy physical formation of her fetus and misses this important formation period. The fetus already has ONSHU when born to this world, because even though he/she chose her as a mother expecting great progress in his/her own spiritual evolution, he/she will have feelings contrary to its expectations because of the mother's ignorance. It is very effective for Self-verification of your mental tendency character, to trace back to your own prenatal life, by directing your consciousness to your mother's womb by the method of "life-regression." What do you feel intuitively?

It is impossible to have the excellent and ideal children they wished for, because parents cannot choose their children, so the only way to have ideal children is by their Self-efforts to raise their own spiritual dimension to conceive a fetus of a relative spiritual dimension.

The PARAREVO theory suggests that the theoretical problems on the earth are that we are not able to explain the true existing purpose and value of the 40 weeks in the prenatal life. Regarding raising children, also, the PARAREVO theory suggests that *it is too late to raise a child after delivering it to this world, so we should raise it in the womb.*

The emerging consciousnesses are the compilation of both spiritual evolution and physical evolution in the evolutionary history, and its foundation will be completed in the womb by directing the spiritual and the physical constitution improvement by the core of love in personality and the core of DNA in the body, according to the "rule of change by birth and re-birth" in the prenatal life.

Chapter Two ☆ The Deriving Point

2-27. Personality formation based on the earth environment

A fetus that has been the collective life entity with the mother will be born from the internal body at the moment he/she leaves the mother's womb and the umbilical cord is cut, and at the time of the birth cry, he/she starts the personality formation for the earth life as one individual life entity.

No matter what your religion or race, and regardless of your status, honor, or wealth now, all humans are born naked and equal. However, the environments waiting after birth are all different, and the personality formation for the earth life will be significantly different depending on what kind of country, ethnic group, or family in which they were born.

For example, the personality formation of a person born in Japan and one born in North Korea will be significantly different because of the difference in the national environment. One who is born in Japan and one who is born in a Jewish nation will be significantly different because of the difference in religion. Also, there will be a huge difference in the personality formations of one who is born to a family filled with love and one who is born to a family with no love. It would be like "the difference between heaven and hell."

2-28. The existing purpose and the existing value in the earth life

Without purpose, is there any reason why we should live for 80 to 90 years on the earth? Since even the prenatal life of 40 weeks has a purpose, which is the preparation for the earth life, there should be existing purpose and value for the earth life. Otherwise the earth life would lose the meaning and significance itself.

Some people say that everything is finished, or everything is gone after you die, however, if everything really returns to nothing, what is the purpose for evolution? If so, it would mean that everything will be completed as nothingness in the end when we die. Everything dies, so the process called evolution would have no meaning or significance, and history itself would be invalid. Also the birth of primitive life entity, bacteria, would have no meaning or significance, because the existing purpose and value of the life itself will be lost.

The purpose and value of the earth life is only the preparation period for the spiritual world, after death. If there is no existence of the earth life, the prenatal life would not be required, and if there is no existence of the spiritual world, there would be no necessity for the earth life at all. And a fetus would never spend time in a prenatal life understanding the earth life, and no one would spend this earth life trying to understand the spiritual world. It is to ensure *the "rule of freedom,"* because the "rule of the universe" makes it possible to continue formation and development eternally by exercising *the principle of independence and freedom.* If the conclusions and results are known in advance, the "rule of freedom" would be lost because we will be dominated by the time axis called future, and the zero time as now, becomes the object instead of the subject, so there would be no meaning or significance for the effect of Self-help, and the "rule of freedom" for Self-Enlightenment and spiritual evolution would fall into dysfunction and recede and cause

Chapter Two ☆ The Deriving Point

personality destruction and spiritual degeneration.

The "rule of the universe" is left to Self-management by Self-determination and Self-completion by Self-responsibility, based on the "rule of freedom," so that no matter good or bad, it completes and lives with the present as a cause. If the "rule of freedom" in the universe is not ensured and freedom would become obsolete, it would be directed to inequality, disorder, and disharmony, so that the entire universe will reach to Self-destruction.

Since people who live the life of PARAREVO are fully aware of the existing purpose and the existing value in life, based on the real view of life and death, they are not spending their time wastefully by directing their precious and irreplaceable life to excessive physical world benefits. They understand that no matter whether they get status, honor, or even wealth, they never achieve Self-completion of the real sense of fulfillment. This is because they understand that fake is fake no matter how it looks. This is the reason so many people feel emptiness and sadness when they get old because people usually live their life like they are running in a marathon without a goal. It will be a totally different and opposite view of life whether you put the existing purpose and values before the goal line of death, or beyond the view of death.

Since our temporal and momentary life of increasing possessions, which we lose eventually, does not go beyond the goal line of the true life, it invites the result to repeat this world again and again, according to the "rule of reincarnation." Therefore, the purpose of this world does not exist in this world but exists in the other world beyond the line of death. This means that there is the existing purpose and value to go to the eternity world, the intangible substantial world, *where we can revel in individual arts of happiness based on free love,* without repeating the inconvenient earth life, many times.

★See diagram "Mechanism of Spiritual Evolution"
on P64, P65

2-29. Earth life determines the spiritual dimension

The environment waiting us on the earth after birth will be significantly different depending on the environment in the mother's womb. It is the same, depending on the spiritual dimension, with the environment in the spiritual world that welcomes the spiritual consciousness entity after leaving the physical body. For example, *whether in the world of the Enlightened Spirit, welcoming us are the Enlightened Spirits who have released the physical domination with love by transcending the "rule of reincarnation," or whether in the world of human spirits, waiting for us are ancestors who are human spirits dominated by the "rule of reincarnation," or whether in the world of ghosts, waiting for us are ill spirits and evil spirits who could not go to the spiritual world even though they shed the physical body and became spirits binding up and trapping themselves on the earth.*

The spiritual dimension is not the world which has been created in the spiritual world. It is the world of mind and spirit which has been created in the earth life by your own self. According to the "rule of the universe," the location of the spiritual world is your responsibility to complete and your determination to manage based on your own free intention. It is because in the spiritual world you have created

Mechanism of Spiritual Evolution

ancestors of physical body

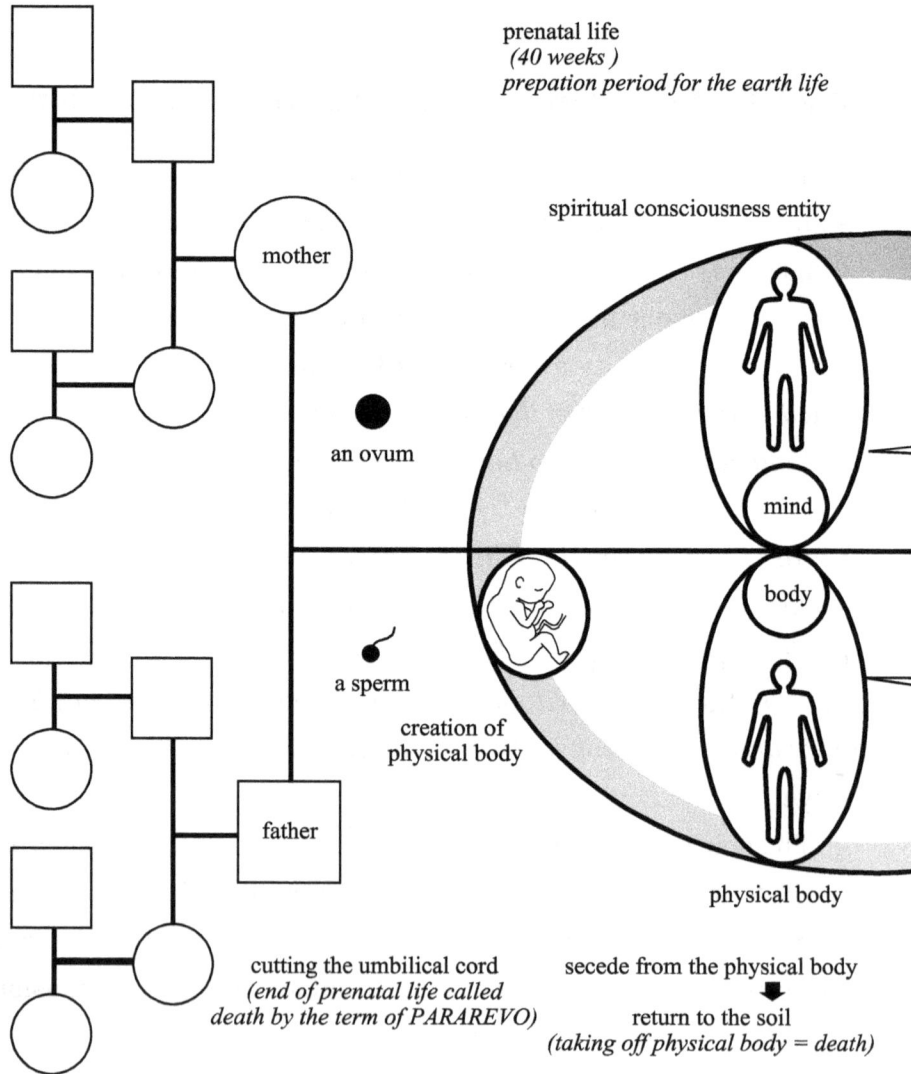

prenatal life
(40 weeks)
prepation period for the earth life

spiritual consciousness entity

mother

an ovum

mind

body

a sperm

creation of physical body

father

physical body

cutting the umbilical cord
*(end of prenatal life called
death by the term of PARAREVO)*

secede from the physical body
⬇
return to the soil
(taking off physical body = death)

life in the cosmic world
(world of light)

the earth life
(approx. 70~80 years)
preparation period for
the spiritual life

to complete true personality formation
to complete true spirituality formation

causal spiritual
decibel world
(Enlightened Spirit Plane)

**the spiritual life
in the intangible earth**

love of
SHINSEI
unity

air • light
food, clothing
and shelter

**the rule of
reincarnation**

mental spiritual
decibel world
(Spirit Plane)

astral spiritual
decibel world
(Ghost Plane)

Chapter Two ☆ The Deriving Point

everything by yourself with Self-determination, so you create either the spiritual world of a higher spiritual dimension, exercising the "soul mind," or the poor demon world of lower spiritual dimension, exercising the "body mind."

Since the environment of the earth life exists as diverse and complex, I mention one of the basic environments for the personality formation, the most influential environment of human beings in common, which is the family environment based on the personality history. It is because the element which becomes the most important and necessary core of love in the personality formation is formed by love from parents, which is the same as in prenatal life.

Since this element is opened by the feeling of love between parents and children as the vertical way, life itself is directly linked to the cause and the result. The relationship between parents and children is the only vertical way. All other relationships such as between wife and husband, brothers and sisters, other human beings, and with all things created in this world, are horizontal.

The life relationship between the parents and children is integrated and connected to the fundamental love of the universe. People who live the PARAREVO way understand the basic system of the vertical love of parents and children, so they form a family to create original and independent arts of happiness based on free love. The basic concept of this major premise is that we must have common existing purpose and values in life so when we live this way, life in the vast and limitless spiritual world is waiting for us.

2-30. Ideal personality formation in the earth life

If the parents have built an ideal family by the PARAREVO way of life based on free love, it should be a family as follows.

As a husband, he wants to live for his wife. He wants his wife to be pleased. Would he be a respectable husband for his wife? Is his wife proud of him as her husband? Is he able to be seen as an ideal husband and an ideal man to her eyes and heart? Is he able to say positively that he lives to please her? It doesn't matter what his wife did or did not do. The biggest concern for him is that he should be an ideal husband and ideal man for his wife. He makes this his purpose of life. To do this, he must establish Self-integration in which he is the subject of himself, and exercise a clear identity to his wife toward the existing purpose of life, so it will be the greatest way to achieve Self-completion as an ideal husband.

Or course, as a wife, she also wants to live for her husband. She wants to see him happy. Would she be a respectable wife for her husband? Is her husband able to be proud of her as his wife? Is she able to be seen through her husband's eyes and heart as an ideal wife and an ideal woman? When husband and wife are holding the same existing purpose and existing value of life in common, and they work together to show the ideal form of husband and wife such as loving and caring for each other, and promoting and understanding each other, so their children are able to achieve the personality formation in the ideal love.

A husband has to complete the role and responsibility of a father to his children and has to become a role model of ideal love. So, it is important that he should be seen as an ideal form and model father to the eyes and hearts of his children. Thus, in the future, if his child is a boy, the boy would think "I want to be an ideal man and an ideal father like my father." Or if his child is a girl, she would think "I want to marry a man like my father."

This is because the father particularly, by the "rule of the negative and the positive" *(all things have an opposite nature and form harmony and order simultaneously and synchronically with slight fluctuation, by the relative original power),* has a significant impact on girls, and girls build up the personal balance of the negative and the positive by love from the father, and when the girls marry they will chose a man from the father's role model image. Of course, the mother has a significant impact on boys according to the "rule of the negative and the positive."

2-31. Emotional relationship between child and parents, and the "rule of relativity"

I have heard that many women have thought they never wanted to marry a man like their father, but it actually often happened that they did marry one just like their father. This is called *the "rule of relativity of consciousness."* By this rule, certain powers such as gravitation, which pulls, and repulsion, which pushes, are derived with something which is being relative, according to its spiritual dimension of consciousness, based on *the "rule of relative field."* And the "rule of relative field" is the fundamental principle in order for power to be derived. If there is nothing to be relative, no power and energy would be produced. The field is formed between the relative things, and the power and energy would be different based on the size of the relative field.

There are many old sayings like "children never listen to what the parents say but will do what the parents do," or "birds of a feather flock together," "they are two of a kind," or "they fight like cats and dogs," "we are like oil and water," and so on. Those expressions are based on this rule.

The "rule of relative original power" shows that we are only able to connect the relativity within the consciousness of our own experiences. Therefore, it will be very difficult for a girl to make a loving and lasting relationship with any man who does not resemble her father. A father should love his daughter sincerely and deeply with his feelings and his heart, and try to keep his daughter from falling into *a lack of paternal love syndrome.* When the daughter lacks paternal love, her personal balance of negative and positive collapses and may direct to personality destruction and mental disorder based on the sexual deviation disorder.

If she falls into this sexual deviation disorder, her behavior may be like one of the following. If her character is inclined to be of a positive nature, she directs her energy to outside, seeking paternal love, and by undifferentiated sexual impulse, falls into sexually disgraced delinquency and becomes sex dependent dominated by sexual desire, having sexual relationships with many different men and/or hanging with a group of unsavory people, or falls into Self-destruction such as drug addiction. If her character is inclined to be of a negative nature, she shuts herself up and becomes depressed, or falls into a negative type of mental disorder like schizophrenia, or becomes a social dropout, or falls into mental disorder like Self-injurious behavior such as slashing her wrists.

Chapter Two ☆ The Deriving Point

A mother also has to fulfill her roles and responsibilities as a mother by showing herself to her children's eyes and heart as an ideal woman, wife, and mother. So, if her child is a boy, he will want to marry someone just like his mother, and if her child is a girl, she will want to be just like her mother. It is important that a mother show herself to her children as a role model of an ideal woman of love for their future goal.

A boy whose personality balance is broken by the lack of maternal love also falls into sexual deviation disorder, and exhibits sexual disgrace by undifferentiated sexual impulse and violent nature by sexual desire domination. And he often joins troublesome groups such as motorcycle gangs or criminal groups and then eventually shows a tendency to expose sexual disgrace behaviors such as sexual crimes and abnormal behavior.

Therefore, it will be important in the personality formation to build a solid emotional and spiritual foundation of ideal love between parents and children. Thus, the root of the social evil is sexual deviation behavior which comes from sexual deviation disorder in the personality formation history between parents and children.

In the way of PARAREVO life, it is a very important concept to build sexual differentiation of a higher spiritual dimension in love between parents and children.

2-32. The ideal family of love, which cannot be built with religion or philosophy

A woman who divorced after eight years of marriage because of the differences in characters between she and her husband, returned to her parents' home with her two children. She asked her parents, "Father and mother, please tell me what is the purpose of our life?" However, her parents just parried her question and said, "What are you talking about? There is no such thing. You must be out of your mind."

Have you ever been taught about the existing purpose and value of life from your parents, teachers at school, superiors in your company, or anybody else? All we hear from religious groups are pray to God, memorial services for ancestors, propagandism, mission work, and offering, and we might be forced into religious activities and other things that have nothing to do with the ideal family of love.

When we look around us, we see there is nothing that exists without purpose. Everything has existing purpose and is directing to complete existing values. Of course, each of us has our own goal of life, however, for some reason no one has found the common purpose of life. The goal is Self-realization of individuality of each and the purpose is Self-completion of the nature of human beings in common. Therefore, *the common purpose for human beings is achieving Self-completion of life.*

Recently, there are many young women who ask serious questions about the real view of marriage such as, what is the most important thing regarding marriage, and what are the conditions for a happy marriage, etc.

A research company carried out a survey targeting the husbands of 8,048 women who were 65 years old or more and live in a typical family. An astounding 68% felt that they are just roommates with their husbands, 12% of them said they did not want to even share

Chapter Two ☆ The Deriving Point

air with him, and 6% of them considered they were living under a condition of domestic separation. It means that 86% of those women surveyed felt uncomfortable living with their husbands and had negative feelings toward him. In this survey, the women were also asked when their feelings shifted. The result was 98% said that when they married they loved each other and were happy, however, after 7 years that decreased to 15%, and then it became nearly 0% after 25 years.

When we seriously consider this, the reality is that such couples are the majority and it suggests that the mechanism of marriage itself has a fundamental error and/or the system of marriage has a serious defect. Why have human beings continued with such an incorrect mechanism and defective system of marriage without questions? It is because of the ignorance of human beings, and the greatest ignorance is to not be aware of the real existing purpose and value of life.

Even if a married couple walks the path of life together, hand in hand, it will not work out unless they aim for a common goal. If they start by walking their own course with totally different purpose and values, their marriage will falter and most likely will end in divorce, or they will live a life of hurt and agony, being dragged unwillingly, and reluctantly struggling, according to the *"theory of hopelessness."* And, as time goes on, such a couple hurt their mind and soul and seriously injure each other, and eventually end their life together holding the unanswered question, "What was the purpose of our marriage?"

Where is the goal of life? It is located beyond the border between life and death, which is called "the verge of life and death," and is the goal line of this world.

Husband and wife would not be able to treat each other tenderly, love each other, understand each other, and nurse each other throughout their life unless they have the common existing purpose and existing value beyond "the verge of life and death." To establish a view of marriage not regretted by mistake, a woman and man have to use their wisdom and recognize the common existing purpose and existing value for life as their firm core and start their life as a couple. Otherwise the real marriage would not materialize. Thus, even though a couple spend their marriage life together on the earth, it would be meaningless if they just live together safe and sound without incident. Even if they say "I love you" every day, it is most likely in a range of Self-satisfaction and narcissism. If their common purpose of the marriage is only to stay together until they separate by death, it is only to satisfy the dietary desire consciousness and the sexual desire consciousness together. Temporal love has a limitation.

When their existing purpose and value in life is directed to a higher level, based on true love, their individuality art will be completed as their mutual joy. If you are a brilliant individual, or even a saint or righteous person, it will be absolutely impossible to complete love alone. You need an ideal partner, woman or man, to complete love. To reach "Heaven," in the universe according to the PAREVO theory, there is a strong, thick and sturdy special spiritual door. When you try to enter "Heaven," the door will not open unless the key and the key-way mesh relatively and exactly. The key to open the door to "Heaven" is given to man, and woman has been given the key-way. The spiritual key is given in the male

Chapter Two ☆ The Deriving Point

genitalia (penis), which is the symbol of man, and the spiritual key-way and the entrance of the door are in the female genitalia (vagina), which is the symbol of woman.

It is impossible to open the door to "Heaven" by the spiritual key of a single man only, or by the spiritual key-way of a single woman only, or if the key and the keyway are mismatched. Also, the door to "Heaven" does not open with the pair of two keys or two keyways. So, homosexual love is the phenomenon of undifferentiated sexual impulse, and according to the PARAREVO theory, is atypical behavior. PARAREVO does not insert abnormal behavior into its theory at all because it destroys the "rule of the universe" itself. Precisely, some humans are connoting their issues and problems in their spiritual consciousness entity to become gay and lesbian. If they are not focusing their own spiritual formation history and personality formation history to re-exam their own assignments, and just abandon Self-responsibility and shift the responsibility to others, nothing will be solved. Since his/her soul selects its own sex before he/she was born, the fluctuation of inner self is big and unbalanced when the soul and the body do not match. It is not the fault of the parents. They should bear Self-responsibility for their Self-determination. The only solution is to make Self-effort to release ONSHU for their sexuality.

This is not only a physical key and keyway for sexual relationship, but is created carefully by the husband and wife throughout their life based on emotional feelings and spiritual true love. The most serious issue for us as human beings is that we do not understand that *the relationship between woman and man is directed and exists by paradoxical theory and value* by the "rule of entropy relativity," which is the most fundamental rule in the universe.

History clearly shows that it is absolutely impossible to build an ideal love for a couple and family with the theoretical framework and value of religion, ideology, and philosophy. It is because saints of the past, such as Jesus, Buddha, and others, were bachelor men and they had never manifested the shape of love and ideal couple as role models to this world, but only expanded male logic, Self-righteously.

The PARAREVO theory is the most existential, easy to understand, and definitely not difficult to follow. The concept is to direct the realization of the world of co-existence, co-prosperity and symbiosis forming ideal ethnic groups and nations by forming ideal societies by building love and ideal couples, and the ideal family becomes the foundation by the way of PARAREVO life.

For people who do not live the PARAREO way, marriage does not have the common existing purpose and values for a life, so most of the couples are not the ones to give love to each other but to seek love from each other. As a result, they have built a marital relationship of sorrow and ONSHU, and share inconvenience by co-dependency and co-domination, according to *the "principle of dependence and domination,"* with empty and momentary values, and end their life because they were just living to live. Since the motive of those non-PARAREVO marriages is not to give love to each other but to seek physical world benefits from each other with calculating values, they inevitably invite catastrophe by drying up their minds, spirits, and emotional feelings. They end up saying, as their catch phrase, "It should not be like this." Such couples would walk a Self-centered life.

Chapter Two ☆ The Deriving Point

A husband who is no longer able to receive love and joy from his wife, turns to alcohol, or gambling, or becomes a workaholic or a womanizer and having affairs with other women because of the loneliness in his heart, and by the *collapse of conjugal love*. A wife, in order to fill her empty heart, becomes a brands addict, infatuated with celebrities, or becomes an obsessed, education-minded mother because her love desire is targeted only to her children, or becomes a religion addict or entertainment addict, or male addict having affairs with men, and in the end, invites the results of domestic separation or domestic divorce or even actual divorce.

Naturally, children raised in these families end up falling into Self-hatred and Self-injurious behavior by Self-denial and Self-escape by *collapse of love between parents and children,* because the parents do what they like rather than what is good for the children. It also causes their personality and mental destruction, and will appear as refusal to go to school, hazing, social withdrawal, domestic violence, delinquent behavior, anorexia, bulimia, schizophrenia or negative type mental illness.

Those are all about sexual deviation behaviors by sexual deviation disorders, which are caused by *lack of love from parents' syndrome,* and appear as impulsive behavior of *confirmation conduct of love,* such as Self-injurious behavior by Self-hatred. In the end, the *confirmation conduct of love* invites family breakdown and family ruination and falls into Self-destruction, destroying the personality balance of negative and positive by its own personality demolition. Foolish mothers drive their children to academic supremacy as a tool of Self-satisfaction and Self-intoxication, or drive them to sports, use them as tools for vanity and appearances, and in the end, fall into DV (child abuses and abusive violence.) They deprive their children of basic freedom, forcing their children to achieve their dreams, which they could not reach by themselves.

All causes are the result of personality destruction and Self-destruction, which are directed by *the lack of love syndrome* as lack of integrity by collapse of love between parents and children, and between wife and husband.

2-33. Emerging consciousnesses and the importance of maternal love

The emerging consciousness is a surface consciousness, which is the same as visible existence like an iceberg floating on the sea. The emerging consciousness is derived from two different personality formation histories. One is formed based on the environment and experience in the womb starting from the moment a sperm and an egg are combined to the moment the child is born to this world. The other is based on the environment and experience on the earth, starting the moment the child leaves the mother's body and makes the birth cry.

The first personality formation is called *the "direct emerging consciousness."* During this period a mother and a fetus are unified and make spirituality improvement which will be the core of love of the emerging consciousness, and improvement of physical condition which will be the core of the body, based on the "rule of change by birth and re-birth." It will be completed by direct maternal love.

The latter personality formation is called *the "indirect emerging consciousness."* It will gradually become independent from the

Chapter Two ☆ The Deriving Point

maternal love to make its own personality formation process under various environments in this world. It will be fostered by indirect maternal love and form a surface part of the emerging consciousness. The reason maternal love has a big influence is that the relative subject is a woman and based on the "rule of the change by birth and re-birth," *only women are given the love and power of creation to be able to conceive life entities, according to the "rule of change by birth and re-birth," and give a birth to this world.* Since men can implant sperm, but are not able to conceive life entities or foster them in a womb and give birth, things which produce and foster lives are symbolically called mother such as mother earth, mother country, etc.

"Direct emerging consciousness," which is a prenatal formation consciousness, and "indirect emerging consciousness," which is an earth formation consciousness, are integrated and form a complex personality. This complex forms a character mentally, and physically it forms a body.

So, which consciousness has a bigger influence on a life? It is the "direct emerging consciousness," which is a prenatal formation consciousness.

The PARAREVO theory suggests that we should understand the real nature of love and that during the prenatal life the mother united with the fetus will raise the kindness personality and compassion of the child. Once a child is born on the earth, parents generously support their child and allow the child to spend his/her life by the child`s free individuality.

2-34. Emerging consciousnesses are the final chapter of consciousness formation

Once primitive life entities were born on this earth star, their consciousnesses started from the instinctive survival consciousnesses, the original existing consciousnesses, and achieved spiritual evolution according to the "rule of reincarnation" based on the "rule of spiritual causality" in 3.8 billion years. It also achieved physical evolution according to the "rule of genetic linkage" based on the "rule of physical causality." And by having changed to the instinctive remaining consciousness, the subconscious, we were able to reach the emerging consciousness in this world. Thus, in any given period, we could say that the emerging consciousness is the collection of the process of the evolutional history and the fruition of evolution.

Since the emerging consciousness represents all history based on the "rule of preservation by inscription," it is the most important consciousness of the three consciousnesses. It means that *all is well that ends well.* No matter what kinds of past consciousnesses or genetic consciousnesses exist, it will be the most important concept, for the way of PARAREVO life, to achieve Self-completion by accomplishing Self-responsibility by Self-determination, in this world.

2-35. Time axis domination by the brain memory

I would like to explain about the "dimension" of this world where we are living. The "dimension" means all axes of coordinates exist

Chapter Two ☆ The Deriving Point

in memories and consciousnesses in the brain. Since a point does not constitute an axis, it is defined as zero dimensions. An axis, which is the assembly of connected points, is called a line and is defined as one dimension, and two axes, which are the assembly of overlapped lines, are called a face and defined as two dimensions. Three axes, which are the assembly of overlapped faces, are called a three-dimensional shape and defined as three dimensions, and we define this three-dimensional structural world of the three dimensions as the material world. In a three-dimensional structural world, the axes called length, width, and height exist; however, we are not present only in this axis of consciousness.

There is another axis of consciousness, which is *the "conceptual axis."* This axis is created by memories in the human brain, and works for the expediency of human beings as the phenomenon of all things in nature as a natural phenomenon by the movement of the sun and moon. This is *the "imaginary axis"* called past and future, which do not exist in the realities of now. Our consciousnesses exist on the "imaginary axis" line called time axis, and past and future exist on the consciousness axis line called concept based on memories in the brain. The consciousnesses dominated by memories in the brain are directed unconditionally to the time axis called past and future.

This is called *the "time axis domination by memories in the brain,"* and everything on the time axis such as status, honor, and wealth will disappear from memories at the same time the spiritual consciousness entity is released from memories of the brain by suffering from brain disabilities such as Alzheimer, cerebral hemorrhage, stroke, dementia, cognitive impairment and traumatic brain injury.

2-36. Human history is a journey of Self-discovery

Verifying the direction of the subject of mind and spirit of human beings, we are able to know a part of the purpose of life.

When you are living only in a beautiful place of sparkling silver and gold surrounded by treasure, and suddenly a flower blooms at your feet, which one attracts your mind more? Is it the silver and gold and treasure, or the flower? Naturally, you are attracted to the flower. Why? You have a closer relationship with plants than minerals because plants have the beauty of life. Like humans, they are born, they live, and then they die.

Then, you are standing in a flower garden which looks like paradise and a cute bunny hops in front of you, which is your mind more attracted to, the flower or the bunny? Your mind is attracted to the bunny. Because being an animal, the bunny is closer in existence to you than plants, based on the view of life.

Now, if you are standing among only strange cute animals and a human passes in front of you, which are you more attracted to, the animals or the human being? You are more attracted to the human being.

Then, you are in a crowd of people and you see your friend pass by, your mind is attracted to your friend.

While you are enjoying time with your friends, you see your parents walking by. When you confirm the presence of your parents, you become uncomfortable with an uneasy feeling which is difficult to explain. It is because you hold the feelings of both love and ONSHU toward your parents. Since their existence tells you the problem and assignment of yourself, you would have complex feelings when you recognize them.

The case with the parents is a little different, but generally, as we see in those examples, we always have interests in and are attracted to the presence closer to ourselves, and if the closer presence is going away from us, we would have more restless and unexplained, uncomfortable feelings. The closest presence to us is our own presence, so our spiritual consciousness entity as human beings has the most interest in our own selves. However, in spite of our desire to know about the existing purpose and existing value for our own selves, our physical eyes and ears are facing toward the outside rather than inside of us, so we care more about evaluation and criticism by others and are losing ourselves.

According to the rule of "body is subjective and spirit is objective," physical senses like eyes and ears are always directed to the outside, however, according to the rule of "spirit is subjective and body is objective," spiritual sense of the spiritual consciousness entity is always directed to the inside, which has the opposite purpose and values. Therefore, human beings are continuing a journey of *Self-discovery* which has been going on throughout a long history.

2-37. Acquisition competition for the evaluation by others and integration disorder

We human beings always direct our eyes and ears to the outside because we are only interested in the outside. We are constantly dominated by appearances and vanity, and living a life like a weathercock, caring about the eyes, ears, and evaluation by others.

For example, I am not going if that person goes, or if this person goes I am going, etc., you are always caring about that person or this person, but really who are you? You are living a life with *an absence of yourself*. You are falling into a "good child syndrome" of acquisition competition for others evaluation and values, so you are going to spend your life as an actor, playing yourself with the theory of `that's the way it goes`. Even though you say that you are living your own life, if you are living to protect yourself by the benefits of this world, you are not living your life for yourself, but for others. The Japanese kanji character "false" is written by two radicals as "for the sake of others."

If we continue such a life, we will be falling into negative feelings and become restless, and suffer from Self-hatred and Self-denial, attacked by mental disorders and/or personality destruction such as depression, and fall into Self-destruction by Self-injurious behaviors such as suicide.

Schizophrenia is the extreme victim consciousness, always suffering from hallucinations and falling victim to delusion such as feeling nonexistent, and believing things like another person is saying this or saying that, or they are doing this or that, etc.

2-38. The existence of SHINSEI, which is the root consciousness

The transcendental root consciousness is like the ocean, which transcends the scope of icebergs, and is also the consciousness which exists in the fundamental world in the universe. This is the

Chapter Two ☆ The Deriving Point

"SHINSEI integration consciousness."

If there is an inherent nature, which encompasses everything equally to the whole of creation, and exists in the vast and infinite universe, what kind of existence is it? According to the PARAREVO theory, DNA is *the common denominator of the physical body for living things on the earth, but also suggests that the common denominator of the spiritual consciousness entity for living things in the universe and the whole of creation is SHINSEI.*

Our soul has prepared for the eternal sustainable system in the spiritual world, as a substance of life with the mechanism, which creates the eternal sustainable power by the relative original power with SHINSEI. SHINSEI, the inherent nature, is *the existence that has the capacity to accept everything as it is, unconditionally and totally, based on free love. It is also the source of power that creates existence and directs every moment of now to a higher spiritual dimension, according to the "principle of dimensional integration" by the relative original power which is derived from the slight fluctuation of imperfection between SHINSEI and the spiritual consciousness entity.*

The purpose of life is finding yourself, and the real Self-discovery is to verify and confirm the existence of the core of the universe, SHINSEI, which is deep inside your spiritual consciousness entity.

In many periods of time and in many lives, we are coming back to this world, according to the "rule of reincarnation," and SHINSEI has always been there together with our spiritual consciousness entity. When we die and come back to this world again, SHINSEI is still there, alive in us, as if nothing happened. Thus, the real Self-discovery is the assurance that we have accepted our existence by the unconditional love of SHINSEI.

We should surpass our memories of resentment ("body mind") of our spiritual consciousness entity, which has been recorded in the instinctive survival consciousnesses (memories of DNA) in our history of past lives, and accept ourselves with gratitude and happiness, unconditionally and totally, by Self-compassion and Self-affirmation of the existence of ourselves, in now. We should release resentment of the memory of the body, carved by the desire of the instinctive remaining consciousness in the evolutional process of the spiritual formation history (soul) and the personality formation history (mind), starting from the "instinctive survival consciousnesses" in the time axis of our history (the past). In order to do this, we must have the courage to release desire and attachment toward the physical world benefits, first.

When we accomplish the way of life as PARAREVO, which is *to make Self-completion by bearing the Self-responsibility to accept the present as it is, unconditionally and totally, with gratitude and happiness by Self-determination based on free intention,* by transcending the sorrow and ONSHU of the spiritual consciousness entity caused by the desire for excessive physical world benefits such as status, honor, and wealth based on material desire and domination desire, which are the instinctive remaining consciousnesses from the genetic domination accumulated in the brain. After that, it would be possible to find SHINSEI, the real Self-discovery.

Thus, the existing purpose and the existing value in this world, is accomplishing Self-completion by Self-discovery. The Self-completion of our life means that we should direct the triangle of SHINSEI, spiritual consciousness entity, and physical body,

Chapter Two ☆ The Deriving Point

from *the dominating structure of ONSHU,* in which the spiritual consciousness entity is dominated by the body, and SHINSEI is dominated by the spiritual consciousness entity, based on the principle of dimensional domination, toward *the integrating structure of love,* in which the body is integrated with the spiritual consciousness entity and the spiritual consciousness entity is integrated with SHINSEI, based on dimensional integration. When we do that, at the moment of our death, when our spiritual consciousness entity is released from our physical body, it will be possible to exist eternally in the spiritual world as SHINSEI integrated life entity by forming the sustainable mechanism to create the power and energy eternally, and by universal love based on the system that is possible to exist as relative original power which is completed into the two-layer structural pair system with SHINSEI and the spiritual consciousness entity.

2-39. True inherent nature existing in the root consciousness

A vector (power and direction) of SHINSEI, inherent nature, always directs to a higher spiritual dimension according to the "principle of dimensional integration." However, even though SHINSEI directs to a higher level, it does not mediate or intervene, ignoring the "rule of freedom." This rule is called the *"principle of nonaggression and nonintervention."*

SHINSEI is integrated to the central intention in the entire universe, and without the past or future, transcending the time axis, it completes perfectly to zero time, now, this moment, and then vanishes. All memories of SHINSEI are removed immediately and overwritten and reserved for new memory of a higher spiritual dimension, and makes it possible to sustain zero time.

The desire we have as the theoretical framework and value on the earth star is to create negative legacy and it is also the system to increase the entropy unilaterally. However, SHINSEI creates the system in which entropy constantly completes its own increase and decrease, at the same time and in the same dimension synchronically and simultaneously, and becomes sustainable according to the "rule of balance," and directs the eternity of the universe to the a higher level. So unlike the earth star system, it does not increase entropy unilaterally.

SHINISEI is the existence of SHOGYO MUJO, Buddhism term meaning "All things are in flux and nothing is permanent," which is the digital world (the world of derivative moments) transcending the analog world (the world of integral integration) of the time axis, and the infinite existence transcending time and space, which completes to zero time meaning no beginning no end, Alpha but Omega, the cause but the result, the beginning but the end. This is called *the "rule of entropy relativity,"* and is the important and core rule of the PARAREVO theory.

The "rule of entropy relativity" is described like this. It will be repeating the phenomenon in which opposite things appear and disappear at the same moment, such as "life and death" or "negative and positive," but when "life and death" appear and life is slightly greater than death, we call this condition "life." Even though it completes each phenomenon instantly, it will continue without interruption, so we say it is a sustained condition.

Although the opposite things exist synchronically and simultaneously, there are also relative subject and relative object, and predominance of subject and object is decided by the relative original power based on the slight fluctuation of imperfection, and the whole is directed by that. When the relative subject predominates and the relative original power is derived, it directs the whole to a higher level, according to the "principle of dimensional integration," and always directs to evolution, creation and generation, forming harmony and order. When the relative object predominates and the relative original power is derived, it directs the whole to a lower level, according to the "principle of dimensional domination," and always directs to regression, destruction, and demolition, forming disharmony and disorder.

The relative subject and the relative object exist according to the spiritual dimension, and between plus and minus, plus is the subject and minus is the object, good is the subject and evil is the object between good and evil, the spiritual consciousness entity is the subject between the spiritual consciousness entity and the physical body, "soul mind" is the subject and "body mind" is the object between "soul mind" and "body mind," between woman and man, woman is the subject and man is the object, and life is the subject and death is the object between life and death, so that the relativity of entropy is constantly directed to a higher relative subject according to the "principle of dimensional integration."

2-40. Limits of the material world on the time axis

Materials existing in the tangible substantial world will inevitably disappear. For instance, even the pyramids, the Sphinx, and the Great Wall will fade away and vanish after tens of thousands of years. Seen from the infinite world, hundreds of millions of years of time existing on the time axis will converge to zero (nothing), and there will be no existence of anything in the material world, because nothing will remain even for a short time.

In the world of atoms and molecules, activities are intensive and constantly changing like the Buddhism teachings SHOGYO MUJO (All things are in flux and nothing is permanent). Time axis coordinate is a delusion created by the concept of human memory in the brain as time and calendars based on the changes of nature, such as the movement of the sun and the moon. In the universe, it does not exist. Viewed from the eternal intangible substantial world that has transcended the time axis, the tangible substantial world that exists in the time axis is seen as, nothing is moving, like a collage.

This world is equal to a virtual world of illusion and delusion (false image world), and *the reality exists in a digital world (real image world), which is the zero time period of now, as the moment.* It is not the concept of memories on the time axis, which is imagined as past and future and does not even guarantee facts, but undeniable facts do exist on zero time period. If there is an existence of past in the universe, accumulated integrally without limitation, the universe will become a trash pile of delusion and illusion of the past, and because of increasing entropy (disorder) infinitely, it will be unable to go forward to the future, and eventually, at the moment entropy turns to a decrease, the universe is going to be diminished and will be forced to go the path of Self-destruction. Therefore, generation and development, called evolution, becomes meaningless and purposeless and will become unsustainable by cutting off the chain of life, so that the existence of the universe itself will be eliminated.

2-41. The basic principle of the Universe

What kinds of mechanisms and systems operate the vast and infinite universe?

Firstly, it is possible for the universe to be sustainable by converting and preserving newer information digitally, based on the "rule of preservation by inscription," which becomes phenomenon in zero time, and disappears.

Secondly, it becomes possible to exist eternally by the digital system of zero time period based on the "rule of entropy relativity," which is: the relative subject and the relative object existing in each suitable spiritual dimension, are constantly directed to a higher subject, according to the "principle of dimensional integration," by the relative original power based on a slight fluctuation of imperfection.

For example, "soul mind" is the relative subject and "body mind" is the relative object between "soul mind" and "body mind," and life is the relative subject and death is the relative object, etc. And according to this rule, those opposite things are appearing and disappearing together, simultaneously and synchronically in the same dimension to form the balance, and directing the "rule of relative field" toward harmony and order, which is called the "rule of balance."

The rule of entropy, which in the natural science represents a condition of chaos, is often used to prove the second rule of thermodynamics. Originally, the rule of entropy is applied to the material world, the tangible substantial world, and does not apply to the world of the spiritual consciousness entity, the intangible substantial world. However, the PARAREVO theory clearly differentiates between the "earth logical evidence" and the "cosmological evidence," so when the rule of entropy is applied here, the theoretical systems between the intangible substantial world, based on the "cosmological evidence," and the tangible substantial world, based on the "earth logical evidence," are verified and proven as opposite, *paradox theory.*

I will explain about the rule of entropy, easily and simply. It was originally based on the "earth logical evidence" on the earth star, which is the planet of water, not from the point of thermodynamics but from the point of philosophical cosmology, with the condition and shape of atoms and molecules in the water.

Presume that the condition of atoms and molecules in room temperature water is the standard condition. When we lower the temperature, atoms and molecules in the water lose their freedom by being regulated, and crystallize becoming ice, and are not able to move. This condition is called the decrease entropy. When we reverse this condition by increasing temperature, atoms and molecules obtain freedom and become gas and move around magnanimously and disorderly. We call this condition the increase entropy.

However, when I replace those rules with the "rule of entropy" based on the "cosmological evidence," the increase in entropy is not an increase of disorder, but is the freedom, release, and diffusion by freeing the energy waves of atoms and molecules. And a decrease in entropy is not a decrease of disorder but an inconvenience, restriction, and condensation when the energy waves of atoms and molecules become restrained. All things in the universe exist, depending upon the spiritual dimension, as opposites, and are directed to form harmony and order constantly in each relative dimension, according to the "rule of balance" and the "rule of relative field," based on the "rule of entropy relativity."

Based on the "rule of entropy relativity," at the moment *plus* derives in the same spiritual dimension, the opposite *minus* derives synchronically and simultaneously. So when we say there is *life,* there is also *death,* good also evil, negative also positive, and "soul mind" also "body mind," they derive synchronically and simultaneously in order to form a balance. Since our "soul mind" and "body mind" are inevitably forced to exist, we are not able to deny the existence of both minds in each spiritual dimension, even a poor personality person or saints and righteous people, like Buddha and Jesus, had both "soul mind" and "body mind."

"Body mind" and evil things do not exist because of the degradation of human beings. They exist because growth and evolution make sustainability eternal. They exist in a slight fluctuation of imperfection between them and "soul mind" and good deed for the spiritual evolution to a higher spiritual dimension, eternally. They are directed to "soul mind" and good deed according to the "principle of dimensional integration," by deriving the relative original power according to the supremacy of the relative subject. Yet, it depends on whether directing to the relative subject, according to the principle of dimensional integration, or whether directing to the relative object, according to the principle of dimensional domination, are left to Self-determination based on the "rule of freedom," and directed to Self-completion by the principle of Self-responsibility.

By the relative original power, based on free love of the relative subject, and transcending the relative object, we have accomplished generation, development and evolution by directing to a higher level.

2-42. Relative subject and the "principle of dimensional integration"

Although all things are forced to exist, according to the "rule of entropy relativity," by the supremacy in the relative subject and the relative object, the qualitative dimensions (the spiritual dimension) and the quantitative dimension (the materials dimension) are directed paradoxically.

For example, good and evil, "soul mind" and "body mind," life and death, spiritual entity and physical body, exist, when good, "soul mind," life, and spiritual entity are the subject, and evil, "body mind," death, and physical body are the object, the relative subject is superior based on the "rule of the universe," and the lower things are directed to a higher level according to the "principle of dimensional integration," and will create freedom and love by achieving generation and evolution. This rule is called *the "principle of dimensional integration" based on the relative subject.* The basic idea of this rule is that the things in a lower level are comprehensive with the ones in a higher level, and things in a higher level integrate with the ones in a lower level by directing to the higher level, and create more freedom, love, and happiness.

The origin of all life on the earth is bacteria. When we discuss which came first between the relative structure of amino acid and DNA, and the spiritual consciousness entity of bacteria, since the fundamental rule in the universe is that the relative subject based on the rule of "spirit is subjective and body is objective," the spiritual consciousness entity is the subject and the cause, and the material entity (the relative structure of amino acid and DNA) is the object, then the original life entity was born in the earth star.

2-43. Relative object and the "principle of dimensional domination"

When evil, "body mind," death, and the physical body is subjective, and good, "soul mind," life, and the spiritual consciousness entity is objective, higher things are restrained by lower things by the "principle of dimensional domination" according to the relative object based on *the "rules of the earth,"* and create inconvenient sorrow and ONSHU according to the "principle of dependence and domination" directed to inconvenience. This rule is called *the "principle of dimensional domination" based on the relative object. The basic idea of this rule is that the things in the lower dimension restrain the things in the higher dimension, and the things in the higher dimension are dominated by the things in the lower dimension, and create worse inconvenience and ONSHU.*

There is a debate as to *whether women or men are subject.* On the earth star, all things have been determined by the male type dominating structure which has directed and built the mechanisms and systems of society, according to the "principle of dependence and domination." Historically women have been forced to believe that they were not able to live without dependence of the economic power of men, and had to bow to the male domination in order to survive economically. There are various discriminations in the world such as racism, ethnic discrimination, regional discrimination, and religious discrimination. The most severe of these is the discrimination against women.

Women and men have opposite theories, based on the paradoxical theory of the "rule of entropy relativity." The theory of women has been governed by *love, integration, harmony, and creation,* and the theory of men has been governed by *power, domination, struggle, and destruction.* The hierarchical dimension in this world is approved and determined by *the "principle of power and domination"* by men, however, the spiritual dimension in the spiritual world is approved and determined by *the "principle of love and integration,"* by women.

I will give a brief explanation of the two typical principles and rules by the paradoxical theory. When our actions are in words and deeds, by good intention with "soul mind" integrating "body mind," it is called *the "principle of Self-integration,"* and when our actions are in words and deeds by evil intention with "body mind" dominating "soul mind", it is called *the "principle of Self-domination."*

When the spiritual consciousness entity directed to freedom by releasing the desire of the physical body, achieves Self-completion by Self-integration based on love, it is called the rule of "spirit is subjective and body is objective," and when the desire of the physical body directs to inconvenience by dominating the spiritual consciousness entity and achieves Self-destruction by Self-domination giving in to resentment, it is called the rule of "body is subjective and spirit is objective."

2-44. The "rule of the relative original power" based on the "rule of balance"

According to the "rule of entropy relativity" based on the PARAREVO theory, in the relative dimension, the increase and the decrease of entropy are contrary to each other. All things existing in the entire universe are derived synchronically and simultaneously and vanish at the same instant, and contain the opposite things as the slight fluctuation of relative imperfection. They are systematized and operated by the mechanism which forms harmony and order based on each spiritual dimension according to *the "rule of the relative original power" based on the "rule of balance."*

In order for existence to function, the opposite things such as negative and positive, creation and destruction, good and evil, and "soul mind" and "body mind," are derived from the relative original power based on the "rule of balance," and are preserved harmonically and orderly and function according to the circulation of energy. Thus, the opposite things build the field based on the "rule of balance," according to entropy relativity, either in the "rule of the universe" or the rule of nature. They are derived from the relative original power and form harmony and order. They are also directing to a higher level and provide a circulation system by themselves to make it possible to maintain generation and evolution.

The rule of the universe is that when one thing is affirmed, the opposite thing derives inevitably and relatively, and completes the "rule of balance" based on entropy relativity. The PARAREVO theory calls this *the entropy relativity and the "rule of relative field,"* and all things are forced to exist by this rule, such as plus to minus, male to female, up to down, stamen to pistil, N pole to S pole, good to evil, sympathetic (adrenaline) to parasympathetic (nor adrenaline), ontogeny to tumor suppressor gene, left to right, front to back, etc.

I will explain this rule by practical examples. A north exit area of a train station is flourishing but a south exit area is not, or a wealthy class lives on the east side of a river but a poverty class lives a cross on the west side, or one partner of a comic duo succeeded but the other went to ruin after a breakup of the duo, and so on. Those examples are often seen as a social phenomenon and are not a question of good or bad, it is because, based on the "rule of entropy relativity," it will turn to the opposite.

The rule of power and energy in the entire universe forms according to *the "rule of relative field,"* and it will determine, by the relative spiritual dimension, the causal power to derive and the qualitative dimension of the energy, and good/bad fortune. This causal power which derived by the relative wave in the spiritual dimension is called *the "relative wave in the spiritual dimension" and the "rule of the relative original power."*

Therefore, all dimensional things existing in the entire universe are forced to exist according to each spiritual dimension by "the relative wave in the spiritual dimension" and the "rule of the relative original power." It is because there is a fundamental cosmic rule in order for the entire universe to exist harmoniously and orderly, directing to the relative subject by the principle of dimensional integration.

Chapter Two ☆ The Deriving Point

2-45. Life creation process on the earth star

The earth star was born as the third planet in the solar system 4.6 billion years ago, and the next 8 million years was the preparation time of the environment for life entities to be born.

The crucial difference between the earth star and other planets is the existence of water. Water becomes vapor and creates a gas as air. Air creates the atmosphere and forms the gravity field by the ionosphere and the Van Allen belt layer. The earth star is a rare water planet which is the only one in the solar system covered by an atmosphere.

So, by the simple relative structure called amino acid and DNA, a physical model for receiving the spiritual consciousness entity to the earth star became ready, and the evolutionary history for life entities on the earth began 3.8 billion years ago with bacteria, a primitive life entity, as an origin.

Since terrestrial life is the life entity in which the spiritual consciousness entity carries the body, it is an inconvenient spiritual life entity that has to shoulder the "dietary desire consciousness" and the "sexual desire consciousness," which are the "instinctive survival consciousnesses," as its fate and has to perform life activities, according directed to the rule of "body is subjective and spirit is objective." As a result, terrestrial life is to the common ecological behaviors according to the common desire consciousnesses, and even if the figure and shape are different from bacteria to human being, their life activities are similar. Both spend their time as labor for completing the "dietary desire consciousness" to live, and perform reproductive activity and raise children, completing the "sexual desire consciousness" for the preservation of the species and the extension of territories, and they will end their lifetime with a way of life for living in this world. So, you could say that terrestrial life is carried out through the rule of "body is subjective and soul is objective," and considers the physical sense as a guide for life.

The bandwidth of the energy wave that can be confirmed by the physical visual range in the human's sense of sight is only distinguishable within the range of a slight vibration wave between 360 nanometers (NM) and 830 nanometers (NM), and cannot be seen as sense of sight. Stars which can be confirmed during the daytime are the sun and the moon only, and the level of the physical visual range cannot confirm other stars. All stars which can be confirmed as stars, by a telescope, are lower dimensional ones which only emit the material waves.

The life entity with the three-layered structure shouldering the body is extremely rare. Most of the spiritual life entities existing in the universe are essentially the two-layered structure of SHINSEI and the spiritual consciousness entity. When the life entity owns the body, it has limitations on its activities, so we could say that the universe is too vast and infinite as an existence place for the material life entity. This proves, as a hard fact, that the universe is not the place to live with the physical body but the place for the spiritual entity.

In the universe, the spiritual dimensions of the energy waves transcending the physical visual range are spreading infinitely, and stars and life entities composed of various energy waves exist endlessly.

Terrestrial life lives desperately by the way of life to live for preservation and persistence of the physical life, and as ants do not care about or even notice the presence of Mt. Fuji, human beings do not pay much attention to the presence of the universe. We have been tamed by the "instinctive survival consciousnesses" and will end our lifetime ephemerally by being preoccupied with the immediate future without knowing the existing purpose and the existing value of life.

Extraterrestrial life definitely exists, however, since they are all life entities of a higher spiritual dimension and have transcended material life, they are never directly involved in the lower dimensional earth star, or infringe on the "rule of freedom" of the universe, in order to *guarantee the fundamental freedom of the universe.* On the other hand, evil spirits in the lower spiritual dimensions interfere without provocation, so bad things manifest immediately and become phenomenon. If we argue the existence by whether they can be seen or not by our naked eyes, which have an extremely narrow wave range in the physical visual range, the argument itself is extremely low level, and unenlightened.

2-46. The earth star is a unique planet

Life entities on the earth star have gone through a very unique birth process. The circumstances for the material body have been prepared in advance, and after that the spiritual consciousness entity, the soul, dwells. The rule on the earth star is operated by the mechanism and system according to the rule of "body is subjective and spirit is objective" with the concept of time axis and separation interval. It is made up of the totally opposite rule from the one in the universe, in all aspects. When distinguishing the life entities on the earth star from the spiritual consciousness entity of a higher spiritual dimension in the universe, we are the life entities tied in the position of inconvenient spiritual consciousness that have to be dressed in a prison uniform called the body.

Since we carry the physical body, we need air and water to live. However, ironically, water creates air and the atmosphere, and body itself is composed of more than 70 percent water, so you could say that the existence of our spiritual consciousness entity is sealed in water. This water and the atmosphere form the gravity field and cover our body. So, the gravity field of the atmosphere created by water lies heavily on us like the iron bars of a prison, and functions as a dominant power over any material, restraint, or repression.

Water is essential for terrestrial life to live physically and materially. It is also a fact that we are the unfortunate presence unable to survive without water, and at the same time, we are forced to inconvenience and dominated by water, according to *the "principle of dependence and domination."* Water plays a role as a guard of the earth star, the prison planet, and actually the spiritual existence in attendance to the water, plays a role and responsibility of the spiritual domination. The spiritual barrier which is the spiritual boundary between the universe and the earth is water. People who have had a near-death experience have confirmed that there is a spiritual world across "the River."

Those who do not know the role and responsibility of water in the earth star, the planet of water, consider water as a gift from God to the earth star as the planet of intellectual life entities, and make water God like, such as wave motion water, magnetic water, ion restoration water, etc. However, those products have been widespread without knowing what the spiritual existence is as a guard responsible in water. So, since the planet of water is an extremely specific existence in the universe, it has a very important meaning and significance in the way we have to live with water.

2-47. Mathematical evaluation leads to competition and domination

The specific presence on the earth star is numbers. Since our living sphere is a material world, it cannot be composed without numbers. Everything is created by numerical formula, and together with the evolution of mathematics, various civilizations have been created and constructed.

The concept of time and the existence of the calendar in the time axis have been created by numbers. Time does not exist because there is time, but is the concept that has been created in the movement of the sun and the moon by the existence of numbers. The earth star is dominated by the numerical concept according to the "principle of material dependence" based on the rule of "body is subjective and spirit is objective."

All things are forced to exist by mathematical evaluation and mathematical character. Such things as qualitative evaluation to the five physical senses and material quantitative evaluation can be replaced by numbers. The science world is constructed with numerical formula, and all life environments are evaluated and controlled by numbers, such as numerical evaluation of economy and health index in medical inspections. Human beings are always dominated by numbers and have continued acquisition competition for numerical evaluation habitually throughout history.

In the universe, all relative phenomena such as life and death, and appearance and disappearance are completed and exist, synchronically and instantaneously, based on the "rule of entropy relativity." They exist digitally according to the "rule of *the attainment of the spirit during life*," in which the presence itself exists but not at the same time, so they are never preserved numerically, and the concept of numbers itself does not exist.

Throughout history, we have been tamed by the material world and made acquisition competition for numerical evaluation intensify under the numerical domination by *the theory of numbers,* and direct to evil competition principles such as academic supremacy principle and economic supremacy principle, and have repeated a history of struggle and destruction many times. Because numbers are the strongest, most restrictive dominating existence for human beings, we should avoid being dependent on the concept of numbers, and try to live the life that does not hold the delusion and illusion of numerical spiritual domination, so it will lead us to releasing evil competition principles and uncomfortable emotions.

2-48. Words and languages are specific presence on the earth star

We have languages as specific presence on the earth star. The mechanism and system on the earth star are operating by the rule of "body is subjective and spirit is objective," so we human beings use languages as a communication tool. Since there is no air in the

Chapter Two ☆ The Deriving Point

non-gravity world of the universe, it is impossible for sound to exist, so there is no need for verbal languages. In the spiritual world, communication is carried out by thought. When a thought occurs it is transmitted to others instantly with sincerity and honesty.

Since the existing purpose for life on earth is preparation to go to the spiritual world, it is important that the mind, and the speech and deed, as an expression of the physical body, are matched and manifested. It is the specific mechanism and the system of the prison planet that can conduct lie and pretense openly, so that no matter how those words are dressed, we do not know what is in their mind.

People who do not live the PARAREVO life, say things unconcernedly and tell lies, and live impassively with composure, by taking advantages because the world of mind cannot be seen from outside.

People who live the way of PARAREVO live for only one purpose, which is as a preparation to go to the spiritual world. So, they pay the greatest concern to expressing the world of mind and the world of speech and deed equally, and make Self-effort to express the world of the spiritual consciousness entity by the consciousness wave from their soul rather than the necessity and importance of words. They are trying to make Self-Enlightenment and spiritual evolution to heal others and the entire created world. They hope that their existence will give peace, gratitude and happiness.

2-49. The earth star performs the role and responsibilities of a prison planet

We human beings have to live against the oppression of the gravitation field because of our physical body. As a result, we are inevitably directed to inconvenience, and since we need lots of physical energy to function here, we must breathe and eat, thus, we carry our destiny on our back and live according to *the "principle of dependence and domination."* If we are the life entity to survive in zero gravity, we do not need energy for activities and movements even with our physical body, so there is no need to acquire great volume of material energies.

We have a fate shouldering the nature of the three-layer structure of SHINSEI, the spiritual consciousness entity, and the physical body. But when we direct ourselves toward a higher spiritual dimension in the spiritual world, it is possible to live eternally based on the *"principle of independence and freedom"* in which you create your own sustainable energies by the "relative original power" based on a pair system of SHINSEI and the spiritual consciousness entity. So, this fact proves that we are nothing but the life entity on the prison planet, because we are not able to live unless we depend on material energies and labor, inconveniently.

However, the habit of taking things for granted is dangerous. In the evolutional process of 3.8 billion years in the gravitational environment of the earth star, the spiritual consciousness entity has been tamed by memories of the physical dominating structure by the genetic domination continuously, so that we do not notice or even feel the inconvenience anymore, and live the way of life, unconcerned, on the prison star, and will "warp shift" (transmigrate)

Chapter Two ☆ The Deriving Point

to the invisible spiritual world of the earth star after we leave our physical body.

We set up tasks for Self-Enlightenment and spiritual evolution in the spiritual world and descend by conception to the earth star, the prison planet, according to the "rule of reincarnation." In this way, we repeatedly come and go between the tangible and intangible star of the earth.

The emotions of love, happiness, hatred and hostility that transcended the five senses of the physical body will exist in the mind and spirit world of sensitivity and sentiment. The senses experienced in the evolutional history are built into the structural arrangement of the brain gene, and the genetic information integrated in the genetic code is set in motion through the brain hormone, then the brain catches the information which feeds back to the nerve circuit as the nerve senses, called the five senses.

All things in the consciousness, and experienced in this world, are existing in the spiritual world. For instance, the world of the primitive era was reproduced in the primitive era, the world of Civil Wars was reproduced in the age of Civil Wars, and the world of the present is reproduced in the present, so each evolutional history becomes phenomenon in the spiritual world according to the "rule of preservation by inscription."

Based on the "rule of entropy relativity," the earth star in the spiritual world and the earth star in the physical world exist synchronically and simultaneously, as do the spiritual consciousness and the physical body, and they are operated by the exact same mechanism.

2-50. The "rule of give and take" on the earth star

Life entities on the earth star are not able to survive without food based on physical domination. In order to obtain food, we have to work, and in order to work, we have to provide our own time and labor. The mechanism and system of terrestrial life is extremely inconvenient because we have no choice but to pay the price for our freedom to obtain food. Without dependence we could not survive, however because of this dependence, we allow the existence of domination and we must shoulder the nature of *the "principle of dependence and domination,"* so, all mechanisms are systematized by the *"rule of give and take."*

Based on the "instinctive survival consciousnesses," businesses from ancient times have started from barter exchange and prostitution, and all basic designs of food, clothing, and shelter have legalized the economic supremacy principle by the mechanism based on *the "rule of give and take,"* and made the society function by enjoying benefits, and directed it to organized social system.

Since the "earth logical evidence" is based on the rule of "body is subjective and spirit is objective," all things are systematized according to the "rule of give and take" which is *a conditional give and a conditional take.* We judge and decide our deeds as to whether we should be involved or not, because of the physical world benefits and the Self-realization, calculating the cost and effectiveness, and planning with the motivation and thought of interests for the loss and gain, by exercising the consciousness of desire. If things are not directing to the physical world benefits and Self-realization, you don't invest time, labor, or money.

Chapter Two ☆ The Deriving Point

The role and responsibility of physical domination on the earth star are restraint of the spiritual consciousness entity and domination by pain from injury and illness by the physical senses, and by insecurity and fear of death, and restricting freedom and intention of love.

The equation of spiritual degeneration, according to *the "principle of domination of ONSHU,"* is that the spiritual consciousness entity is dominated by the physical body which is a lower dimension than the spiritual consciousness entity, and the physical body directs the spiritual consciousness entity to inconvenience and negative feelings, so that by *the "principle of dimensional domination" based on the rule of "body is subjective and spirit is objective,"* "body mind" dominates "soul mind" and directs the consciousness to a lower spiritual dimension. Because the spiritual consciousness entity is constantly tormented by threat from physical domination and negative feelings and by being frightened of pain from illness and accidents or uneasiness and fear of death, the consciousness has been dominated and tamed. So we are forced to a life of being subordinated by the physical body, continually, as we have been throughout the history of 3.8 billion years.

2-51. The "rule of give and give" of the universe

In the "cosmological evidence," all things are systematized by *the "rule of give and give,"* which is just giving unconditionally and immediately leaving everything behind, based on the rule of "spirit is subjective and body is objective." In other words, this rule is the great virtue of unselfishness by Self-sacrifice.

People, who live the PARAREVO way, exercise the consciousness of love and carry out speech and deed with the creation of happiness as a motivation, and achieve Self-completion. Those who live the PARAREVO life do not decide relationships by evaluation of others, such as wealth or poverty, good people or bad people and superiority or inferiority, etc., but direct their consciousness to create joy for themselves and for all people and material things, by the real love of SHINSEI.

Since the "cosmological evidence" is based on the "rule of the attainment of the spirit during life," all things complete at this moment, zero time, and direct to a higher spiritual dimension by the "rule of preservation by inscription." So, everything completes with love and happiness and disappears, according to the "rule of give and give." People who live the PARAREVO way clearly understand that the existing purpose for life is Self-Enlightenment and spiritual evolution, so they know how to go up the steps of the spiritual dimension.

The equation of the spiritual evolution, established according to *the "rule of change by birth and re-birth,"* means that you should release your ONSHU by loving your ONSHU, and also transcending your inner "body mind" by your "soul mind" which directs you to a higher spiritual dimension, then you will achieve Self-completion by *the "principle of dimensional integration" based on "spirit is subjective and body is objective."*

In order to direct yourself to a higher spiritual dimension, you should pour your love generously and unconditionally with gratitude and joy as *giving everything and leaving everything behind*, based on the "rule of give and give." Then you are able to release from

Chapter Two ☆ The Deriving Point

your "body mind" and are directed to a higher "soul mind."

Even if you give something more important than your life to someone, but the person you gave it to threw the gift in the trash right in front of you, people who live the way of PARAREVO will achieve Self-completion to the consciousness and motivation toward the fact of giving, and will leave it up to the recipients spiritual dimension as to how they treat the gift. They draw the separation boundary line between themselves and others and have no empathy or negative feelings.

The rule of earth is *to demand all things with greed and complete all things with sorrow and ONSHU* based on the "rule of give and take," and then complete your life for the physical world benefit, which you will lose eventually.

The rule of universe is *to give all things with love and complete all things with gratitude and happiness* based on the "rule of give and give." You will then complete your life for the spiritual world benefits which you will never lose, eternally.

2-52. The prison on the prison star (earth) is a geriatric hospital

In the natural world, everything is born naturally, lives naturally, and dies naturally. However, today, human beings are born unnaturally, live unnaturally, and die unnaturally because of the development of medical science.

The theoretical framework and values for life and death on the prison star are directed based on the rule of "body is subjective and spirit is objective," so we are consistently hoping for immortality, wishing to live longer in this world, even if for only one minute or one second, desiring to maintain or cause to maintain the physical life.

Today, with the technology of life-prolonging treatment, it is possible to keep even critically ill people alive for a long period of time. People can continue to live, even though one is not able to eat at all, by sending nutrients to the stomach by intubations if the internal organs are destroyed. And life prolonging treatment is available, even though one is not able to breathe independently, by securing blood circulation and respiration by artificial cardiopulmonary.

Even a death-row convict in prison is given the minimum free activities including eating and walking. And moreover, he is given the time before his death, in which he is able to prepare his mental attitude toward death and time to examine himself for Self-completion.

However, patients who are given life-prolonging treatment in geriatric hospitals do not have the freedom to choose their own time to die but are forced to live, like a living corpse, no matter whether they wish to live or not. They only have pain and hardships forced on to their spiritual consciousness entity, and they live meaninglessly and purposelessly, because of the wrong view of life and death. If you are forced to stay alive, like a living corpse, at first, your relatives and the people who take care of you are fine, however, after a long period time they get tired of caring for you and may begin saying unpleasant things that you do not want to hear, and you have to continue to live in hell on earth, tortured and humiliated, for many years.

People, who think that their life-realization is just obtaining the excessive physical world benefits do not believe in the presence of the spiritual world, consequently most of them feel that everything will be over when they die and everything will return to nothing. Those people have a tendency for a strong attachment to the physical life in this world, but for some reason, they do not allow their life to end peacefully. In order to stay alive, they take life prolonging treatments for many years using their economic power, but eventually they are forced to live in their own created hell because of the advanced life-prolonging treatments, and will leave this world in pain and agony by holding the ONSHU of negative feelings. They have to die in the worst condition and personality dimension, with hate and pain, at the last chapter of life.

Since the purpose of this world is not Self-realization for the excessive physical world benefits, but Self-completion for the spiritual benefits by the way of PARAREVO life, the spiritual dimension will be determined at the moment of death which is the compilation of one's life in this world. Therefore, geriatric hospitals are the worst prisons of severe hell on earth, worse than actual prisons on the earth.

Are doctors in geriatric hospitals, who do not understand the real view of life and death, guards of the prison in hell on earth? If you do not establish the real view of life and death securely, the worst scenario will wait for you in the final chapter of your life.

2-53. The degree of freedom of consciousness and the degree of acceptance of love based on spiritual dimension

To develop our sixth sense, we have to transcend the five

physical senses, vision, hearing, taste, smell, and touch, and direct the consciousness entity, which is contained in all things, and the relative original power to the world of sensitivity and feelings integrated with love and happiness, and manifest it as the individual art. The sixth sense is the world of sensitivity and feelings, beyond the sense of vision to see the beautiful scenery, beyond the sense of hearing to listen to great music, and beyond the sense of taste to taste delicious cuisine.

For example, when we are suffering from terrible sadness or painful feelings and our heart feels heavy and worn out, we are not able to be pleased by the physical senses even if we see beautiful scenery, listen to great music, or eat delicious foods, instead, we amplify sadness and pain. Conversely, when we are filled with happiness that makes us feel like jumping for joy, we can be pleased by whatever we see, hear, or eat. This is because the sensitivity and feelings of the spiritual consciousness entity, the sixth sense, are far beyond the physical senses.

The bandwidth of the relative energy wave in our physical senses only catches a few narrow bands of energy, as though it does not exist, when seen from the energy wave in the universe. The bandwidth of the relative energy wave of visible light in our vision can only distinguish within the range of a few narrow bandwidth of energy waves from 360 nanometers (NM) to 830 nanometers (NM), and does not catch clear vision. Even the speed of light vibrates slowly (300,000 miles per second) compared to the distance interval of the vast and infinite universe. Also, the relative energy wave of sound in our sense of hearing is from 20Hz to 20kHz, and the velocity of sound is about 340 meters within 15 degrees C. temperatures (one

Chapter Two ☆ The Deriving Point

atmospheric pressure per second), so the acoustic sound wave is extremely slow. Even dogs, dolphins, and bats can hear ultrasonic sound waves beyond the human hearing range.

The wavelength range of the relative energy wave between the relative universal original power and the intangible substantial world is the world of energy wave called the super relative wave and is far beyond the velocity of light. It is the high dimensional spiritual light wave world in which the high energy wave vibrates and moves at a terrific speed, far beyond the wavelength range of visible light waves seen by the naked eye. Not only electromagnetic waves such as X-ray and γ-ray, but also infrared light and ultraviolet rays are not able to be seen because they are invisible rays, in the sense of vision. Since nocturnal animals are different in the vision decibels from human beings, it is possible for them to see even in darkness, and the eyes of deep-sea fish function even in complete darkness. Therefore, it is no exaggeration to say that we human beings have a condition likened to visually impaired, who are not able to see the energy wave (light) existing in the universe at all. When we see the universe with the naked eye we only see the world of darkness.

The energy wave in the universe is the ultra-relative wave of unlimited spectrum, beyond visible light, which is filled with a sense of energy, created by unimaginable and infinite energy, so it becomes possible to be relative once the relative wave matches, and becomes phenomenon immediately by the relative original power, even though it is separated up to far in the distance in the universe.

Since the energy details and the height of the wave are different, people who are in a lower spiritual dimension and have negative feelings, are not able to see beauty but only a faded collage even of the most beautiful things in the world, and for them, wonderful music sounds like noise, wonderful scents smell bad, and delicious food tastes terrible. It is because the spiritual world is the relative world in which all things become phenomenon, due to the spiritual dimension of the person himself/herself.

For people who have evolved their spiritual consciousness entity to a higher level in the universal dimension, the best of the best things on the earth by the physical sense in the material dimension, would become meaningless. The degree of freedom and the criterion of love in the spiritual world, where we are planning to go, will be determined by the cause of the personality dimension and the spiritual dimension of each person, according to the relative original power with the relative wave in the spiritual dimension.

2-54. Energy wave level in the spiritual dimension

According to the relative wave in the spiritual dimension, the qualitative dimension of the relative original power to be created will be different on a large scale.

The energy wave of *the "Astral spiritual dimension," the "ghost plane,"* simply shifts from the physical world of the earth star to the spiritual world of the earth star, only by losing the physical body, but its relative wave seldom changes. In fact, a low-dimension psychic who is relative to the wave of residual haunting mentions something about ancestors or last life, just like an extension of this world.

Since the energy wave of *the "spirit plane," the "Mental spiritual dimension"* could not transcend the energy wave of the earth level,

Chapter Two ☆ The Deriving Point

it is not able to transcend the range of the energy wave in the earth star even though it is much more brilliant and vibrant than *the "Astral spiritual dimension."*

The energy wave of *the "Enlightened Spirit Plane," the "Causal spiritual dimension,"* has a huge difference in the thickness and the height of the wall of the spiritual dimension compared with *the "Astral spiritual dimension" and the "Mental spiritual dimension."* The spiritual dimension of the energy wave of *the "Causal spiritual dimension"* is an incomparably magnificent and beautiful energy wave, emitting bright dazzling light and coming and going without bounds and filled with a sense of pulsing energy.

Even though we are not able to see those energy waves, it is reckless and nonsense to argue the existence itself by discussing visible or invisible in the scope of the visible light range of the physical range. Since the things seeable with our naked eyes are equal to nothing, and most things are invisible to us, it is the same as seeing with a visual disorder. Various things such as atoms, molecules, and electric current do exist, however, it is a reality that nobody has seen and confirmed them yet. Most scientists and many other people believe that light and heat emitted from the sun reaches to the earth, although brilliant scientists in the natural science field understand this is impossible.

It is physically impossible for the quantity of light and heat which are attenuated by contrary multiples, to travel for such a long distance through space, which is extremely close to the absolute zero degree, and not lose its strength. When we climb high mountains like Mt. Chororanma, Mont Blanc and the Matter horn, we should feel hot because we are closer to the sun and the temperature should be higher. However, the higher we climb and closer to the sun we get, the colder we feel. So, it is not by the physical light or heat, but by the relative original power between the energy wave of the high spiritual dimension of the sun and the atmospheric density of the low spiritual dimension of the earth star. Thus, the earth environment has been made by light conversion and thermal conversion of the sun's energy to a lower-dimension by being relative with earth.

Since the atmospheric density is more intense on flat ground and thinner in higher mountains, it is natural that the conversion efficiency of light and heat is different, and the difference between summer and winter is caused due to the difference in the conversion efficiency by the atmospheric density in the angle of the solar energy wave.

It does not become phenomenon by unilateral or one-way energy of the sun, and not because a thing reacts or causes a phenomenon individually, but all things become phenomenon in the interactive relation by the relative reaction in the universe, so that the earth environment is created and becomes phenomenon according to the "rule of the relative original power" between the sun and the earth. Since it is the world of the ultra-relative wave, which is far beyond the range of our visual wave and the range of our auditory wave, it is not possible to see or hear by the senses because the channel does not match with the relative wave range of the physical senses.

In the spiritual world, there is no air as a medium for sound (the Doppler Effect) which is the material wave of the worldly level, so even words do not exist. If we go to the universe space with the physical body, we only see the world of complete darkness and complete silence, so we would feel as if we are becoming visually and hearing impaired.

The spiritual wave of feelings and senses transcend the material energy wave and exist in the world of the ultra-relative wave, which is integrated by the relative universal original power based on free love. Communication that uses minute density spiritual base as energy medium can transmit and be received immediately after thought just with the thought and can transcend the speed of light. There is a huge difference between the earth star, which uses air and material as energy medium, and the universe.

We can understand how the physical body catches the wave range dominated by the lower dimensional narrow range, as senses and interchanges, because it can only catch it by faint electric current, which is the neurotransmitter in the physical sense. It is easy for personality and spirit to become lower dimensional by poor relative original power, but is very difficult to become higher dimensional. The high dimensional dark energy wave in the universe changes to low dimensional by phased relative original power, connecting the relative wave with the lower dimensional earth star, and is granulated from ultra-relative particle to dark matter such as top quark, and finally materializes. This proves that how low dimension the earth star is.

2-55. Earth logic is legalized by the principle of domination

The physical senses should be integrated into the spiritual feelings and sensitivity called love and happiness.

The purpose in the rule of the universe is to find the existence value, i.e., *the love of SHINSEI, which is the verity of the individual entity (never changing the truth of the universe which integrates with unlimited freedom and love), and the happiness of the spiritual consciousness entity, which is one's own individual mental entity, are integrated to the unity of SHINSEI, and open the path to feelings, and then manifest the individual art of the high spiritual dimension by directing them to the entire purpose of the universe.*

The sixth sense is the mind and spirit manifesting the individual art of happiness based on free love. However, as the prison planet, the earth star, the spiritual consciousness entity is dominated by unique physical senses based on the five senses, and all functional forms are systematized.

Originally, *the spiritual consciousness entity is supposed to be integrated by SHINSEI, and the body should be integrated by the spiritual consciousness entity, however, all problems are caused because the body dominates both of them.* This system legalizes the theory for domination and has made a course as a valuable matter for the physical world, and exists as the fact that has strengthened the evil competition principle throughout history. For terrestrial life, all things are directed to inconvenience by the "instinctive survival consciousnesses," and legalized by *the "principle of dependence and domination."*

The greatest inconveniences for human beings are *labor and marriage*. They are inserted into DNA, as labor (to live) and marriage (to preserve race). A husband supplies labor for his family and a wife takes charge of child rearing and housework for preservation of the species. For life activities and preservation of the species, man and woman depend on each other, and end up with

Chapter Two ☆ The Deriving Point

the life for just living with inconvenience as its price. As you can see in this system, all things have been directed and legalized to inconvenience, and the social system also has been polarized to both dominate and subordinate, so that in a household, the domination structure that the husband controls the economy and makes his wife depend on him economically has repeated continuously throughout history and the status of women has been severely oppressed. In Hindu and Islam, discrimination systems such as polygamy and caste still exist and are openly carried out in the framework of religious theory.

The pyramid type of social structure has been built by the legalized domination systems such as, mother has privatized her children and ruled legally, husband has been legally ruled by his company in exchange for economy, and companies have been legally ruled by bureaucratic mechanisms by government regulations. Thus, the system has been created legally where the subordinates always have to provide freedom and labor to the dominating side, and in return, obtain the foods for living.

In the prison star, in order to maintain control prisoners, harmony and order, under legal domination, are maintained by the pyramid type of social structure with the dominate side taking from the subordinates side. So, the center of desire in the genetic domination of the dominating side, which has controlled throughout history, is integrated in the brain, and sometimes the brain becomes the driving force that takes charge of thought and desire beyond instinct.

Throughout history, human beings have been able to reign over the top of the food chain of terrestrial life using the brain as a tool, and even through the changes in the earth environment, the knowledge that has strongly survived in the process of evolution by accomplishing environmental adaptation and reaching the summit of the evolutional process, exists in the genetic integrated circuit in the brain.

2-56. Environmental adaptation is a driving force for evolution

The strong challenged harsh environments and went the path of destruction while the weak have done the survival and preservation of species by accomplishing environmental adaptation. In other word, the evolutional process has been led by the weak. Even in the age of dinosaurs, the weak creatures survived by accomplishing environmental adaptation while dinosaurs became extinct in a cataclysm of nature.

For example, the mammoth challenged the severe winters of the frigid ice age, and survived, overcoming the coldness by their thick hair covering, however, in the end, they were annihilated without overcoming nature. Apes overcame the coldness by discarding the hair, paradoxically, and acquiring the wisdom to wear clothes and use fire, so they succeeded in survival and the preservation of the species. With that, apes obtained the greatest tools of wisdom and established the foundation for evolution, and with wisdom as the driving force for evolution, apes succeeded in evolving to human beings, which rein over the top of the life entities of the earth star. If apes had continued wear hair as they used to, the process of evolution would be significantly delayed. *The paradoxical attempt*

Chapter Two ☆ The Deriving Point

of giving up hair in the ice age produced the tool called wisdom and they could use it as the driving force for evolution.

During the ice age, various life entities evolved rapidly by overcoming the harsh environment, and among them, apes achieved the most revolutionary evolution. It is no exaggeration to say that an unconditional acceptance of the weak for severe environmental changes, rather than the strong, created the wisdom for environmental adaptation and became the driving force for evolution and led history directing to the preservation of life.

Also, in the Warring States Period, powerful warriors could not survive in the natural environment because of starvation, but farmers, as the weak, had the wisdom and independence to survive.

We can say the same things about the environmental adaptation in the spiritual evolution. When you encounter severe and poor environment with trials and tribulations, you might want to shift the responsibility by the victim consciousness. However, by "paradoxical attempt," you can accept that environment with gratitude and happiness, totally and unconditionally, as it is, and overcome the hardships mentally and spiritually with the thought of "thank you for the hardships," and you will certainly produce Self-Enlightenment and spiritual evolution.

2-57. Wisdom and desire are a bipolar structure of the brain

The core of our wisdom and desire is located in the brain, and by controlling the central nervous system through the brain cells by the over concentration of the genetic domination, the brain controls the hormonal and peripheral nervous system and has succeeded in controlling cells in the entire body. This means, the brain has total authority over the center of the instinctive survival consciousnesses by genetic supervision, and controls the opposite wisdom and desire of the bipolar structure based on the "rule of entropy relativity," and has obtained the desire dominating structure in order to rein over the top of evolution on the earth star.

The genetic information inherited continuously, in accordance with the "rule of the genetic chain," is preserved as the new evolved information by the "rule of preservation by inscription" in the structural arrangement of the brain cells by the rearrangement of the genes. The original brain plays a role as the center for life maintenance as the retention of old ideas while the new brain is expanding by spreading out to the periphery, so it has made human beings evolve up to the present under the "principle of dimensional integration" by creating new wisdom and desire as a bipolar structure.

For example, the cells of the sole never manifest the desire consciousness. The brain controls our five senses of vision, hearing, taste, smell, and touch which are all dominated by the neural circuit of the brain, and the brain analyzes various senses, and controls the whole body by supervising each and every organ. All pleasures and earthly desires in the excessive physical world benefits will be manifested by the control of all brain cells, so at the moment the brain dies all senses and desires will disappear.

The fact exists, throughout history, that the dominating power has been delegated to a handful of avaricious and intelligence people who have reigned over the top of the social framework, and ruled

Chapter Two ☆ The Deriving Point

society. Desire transcends reason called wisdom. For instance, police and military, which are symbols of the state power, have built the pyramid type dominating structure that legally dominates by putting intelligence groups at the top, and using the rank system and the discrimination system they evaluate humans by rank and superiority. The organization reigning over the top of desire is the central government, and by a handful of intelligence people won out in the end to the evil competition in accordance with the academic supremacy doctrine, the pyramid type dominating structure has been built by legalizing the bureaucracy dominating mechanism. Throughout history, ordinary people have been dominated by such groups. The requirements for reigning over the top are intellectual abilities and extraordinarily strong sexual desires in the bipolar side, and without both of them, it is difficult to be at the top of the dominating structure.

Naturally, the world economy is also dominated by a handful of wealthy people, and the majority remains poor. Take the health care reform in Japan, for another example. A handful of greed and vested interests groups try desperately to protect the interests for those engaged in medical treatment rather than public health, so the Japanese national finances are on the verge of collapse by breaking the primary balance of state budget, significantly.

2-58. Science civilizations lead spiritual culture

With the conflict and agony in the two largest desires of the instinctive survival consciousnesses, we human beings have created the theoretical frameworks and values of religions by using every possible scheme and trick freely. By brainwashing us, cleverly, using both carrot as bait, and stick as threat, religions have directed us to a trap, with fear and terror, and built the pyramidal dominating structure continuously strengthening the centripetal force to restrain the freedom of the faithful by the concentrated authority and dominating power of religious leaders.

The center of the physical desire domination is the brain, and the center of the national desire domination is the central government and it`s agencies, and the center of the brain desire domination is religion by switching domination to spiritual civilization. The nation and the people are dominated by the prison master called the central government and it`s agencies. Companies are dominated by the prison master called the president, and religious groups are dominated by the prison master called religious leaders, so that in each organization and group, each prison master reigns.

They only suggest immediate physical world interests, but do not suggest the real view of life and death to each individual seriously, nor do they specify the existing purpose and the existing value of life, nor point us in the right direction. Which direction are those prison masters going after death?

Even under such conditions, history has certainly evolved, and we have been released from severe labor and inconvenience in the physical dominating structure.

The fundamental rule for evolution is how much we can shorten time and distance, and release ourselves from the time axis, so when we are able to complete all things to restore to the moment of zero time, as now, we are able to obtain real freedom. In order to do so, human beings have built civilizations unconsciously, and

Chapter Two ☆ The Deriving Point

since the Renaissance, have achieved remarkable development of "material civilization."

In particular, in August of 1945, the atomic bombs were dropped on Hiroshima and Nagasaki. After that, science technologies remarkably progressed and we are now blessed with the highly advanced material civilization. Also, July 20, 1967, was a historical moment for human beings. The Apollo 11 space craft made the first landing on the moon and Captain Neil Armstrong took the first step on the moon. He was the first human being in history, wearing the physical body, to stand on the moon. Now is the era when human beings go to the moon routinely. Not long ago, the moon was just a far off existence in fairy tales.

There was a famous message from Captain Neil Armstrong, after he returned to the earth star. He said, "I met God in the moon." He never mentioned before that he met God on the earth star even though he was a devout Christian. This is an important episode to prove that the earth star is "the prison planet." When we are released from the prison star, and transcend the atmosphere of the gravity field, a totally wonderful world in a different dimension opens up to us. The presence which Neil Armstrong met on the moon was not God, but spiritual residents of the moon. They are the life entities living as the spiritual consciousness entity only, without the physical body, in a high spiritual dimension.

Many astronauts had experiences in the universe which shifted and transformed their consciousness. By encountering the spiritual life entities in the higher spiritual dimension, they had various personal experiences and paranormal phenomena, in different dimensions, so that their spiritual consciousness entities caused trans-personality (denatured consciousness) phenomenon and became religious, or started to devote themselves to the spiritual world, or tended to go into a trance, after returning to the earth star. Those are the phenomena caused by the relative original power based on the mind and spirit with the spiritual consciousness entity in the higher dimensional wave in the universe.

2-59. The universe is penetrated by the principle of integration

In the universe, there are numerous life entities that are a higher spiritual dimension than those of the earth star; however, entities in a higher dimensional plane never interfere with those in a lower dimensional plane. It is against the "principle of no aggression and nonintervention" of the universe, and if the "rule of freedom" is ignored, freedom in the universe could not be guaranteed.

All sorts of time and distance in our life circle have shortened, thanks to the development of science and technology, and it has resulted in significantly reducing our labor forces, so we are able to have many conveniences and benefits. The material civilization has taken part in releasing of time and labor by the development of science and technology, as a driving force, so the development and improvement of science is essential to evolve the material civilization and release labor quantity and time axis.

Unfortunately, the spiritual evolution has not progressed like the material civilization. It is still dominated by the theoretical frameworks and values of the past, such as the Bible, Buddhist writings and other scriptures, as the retention of old-fashioned ideas. As a result, the spiritual consciousness entity has not yet established the real freedom, and we are still dominated mentally, following religious and philosophical paradigm and concept, over thousands of years. As the driving force for the spiritual civilization, religion and philosophy were supposed to play the central role and responsibility, however, hypocritical religions do not have any meaning or significance anymore, in modern times. The great lies of the religious theory have been explicated and clarified by the development in genetic engineering, but it is now transforming into a dangerous existence.

Science and technology, which are responsible for the material civilization, and religions that are responsible for the spiritual civilization, have so many differences, distances, and gaps in the evolution history. The controversy between the evolution theory in genetic engineering and the Creationism by God in religious doctrines was solved when Pope John Paul II accepted the evolution theory in 1996. The evolution theory became established by the victory of science and technology, and Creationism has faded out as a false theory.

The PARAREVO theory suggests that the spiritual civilization has been left behind by the material civilization, and the distance between them is becoming greater. With the collapse of religious theories, a highly volatile situation between Christianity, Judaism, and Islam, the crises of nuclear war would become real.

Although we could shorten the distance of the time axis by the evolved material civilization, and release from labor quantity, the spiritual consciousness entity has not yet been released from the instinctive survival consciousnesses, and remains unchanged. So we human beings, like ants, cockroaches, and beasts, even though our shape is different, do the common ecological activities dominated by the common desire consciousness and will end our life time just living a way of life for living. If the material civilization unilaterally accomplishes evolution but leaves the spiritual civilization behind, like right now, eventually the two civilizations will lose the integration, and the spiritual civilization will become dominated by the material civilization. This will necessitate the earth star to do choose the path to destruction because of the irresponsibility of religions.

Essentially, the spiritual civilization has to be the subject and build the material civilization as the object, and by integrating the body into the mind, direct it to a higher spiritual dimension to form harmony and order. So we have to construct the society and the world, which have the capabilities to develop both civilizations together. However, we have the historical circumstances and facts that the material civilization has proceeded and led the spiritual civilization since the origin of life, based on the rule of "body is subjective and spirit is objective." As a result of building the history of the material civilization before the spiritual civilization, which is totally opposite from the rule of the universe, our world is in a critical situation at the present, because it is an undeniable fact that the material civilization has developed the atomic bomb and hydrogen bomb, indicating the possibility to totally destroy the earth star.

The year 1995 was a significant year for our history. It was the year that the world population reached 5.67 billion, Islam possessed nuclear weapons, and the 50 years anniversary since the atomic

Chapter Two ☆ The Deriving Point

bomb was dropped on Hiroshima and Nagasaki. And after 1995, the spiritual civilization was pushed into the corner by the material civilization. We are now confronting the era of decline, and have gone beyond the point of no return.

The role and responsibility for religions on the prison planet, throughout history, have been to talk about God, saints, the spiritual world, ancestors, so earthly desires for human beings have theorized untrue theories as religious doctrines, and the human being has become the human god. They brainwashed the people and preached false teachings to dominate and utilize legally for the worldly domination and benefits. Thus, we could say that religions play the role and responsibility as a guard to keep people on the prison star. The rule of the universe is operated by the rule of entropy relativity and is directed to the relative subject by the principle of dimensional integration, and superscripted genetic information to a higher spiritual dimension, and accomplished evolution.

The Bible, Buddhist writings, and other scriptures are made by past facts, which are *the existence of the phenomenon based on the events,* and at the present time, have not even reached to the facts or truth. Men of religion and leaders of new religion groups claim that the Bible and scriptures are the eternal truth and consider them as absolute. The word "absolute" exists in our life, but there is no absolute in the universe and all things exist relatively. If one absolute truth exists, why are there hundreds of new religions born one after another?

Nobody went to the moon and there was no atomic bomb or hydrogen bomb existing in the era of the Bible or The Buddhist writings. If there had been, in the time when Jesus or Buddha was alive, it was the lower spiritual dimension in their background, so the earth would have already been destroyed.

By the rule of the relative wave and the relative original power based on the spiritual dimension, along the time background accompanied with the spiritual evolution, wisdom, called invention and discovery, had been given to the person who played a role and responsibility, and the material civilization achieved evolution synchronically.

Religious organizations and groups in the world are not able to correspond to changes in the material civilization because of their Self-righteous interpretations, so they are being used as a tool of desperate terrorism by fundamentalists, fanatical believers and unquestioning believers.

2-60. Now is the era when the Christian Bible, Buddhist writings, and other scriptures begin to fade

Hundreds of different denominations of religious organizations have been derived from the Christian Bible, Buddhist writings and other scriptures, according to each Self-righteous interpretation. For instance, there are Catholic, Protestant, Presbyterian, Mormon, and Jehovah's Witnesses, which are all derived from the Christian Bible. Buddhism is the same. There are many denominations, such as Zen-shu, Nichiren-shu, Sodo-shu, and Shingon-shu. If these had reached to the universal truth, all things should have been integrated and completed in one truth.

However, even though the presence of phenomenon based on certain things is only one fact, there is the truth, which is the

Chapter Two ☆ The Deriving Point

presence of consciousness based on SHINSEI, exists in numbers of consciousnesses in each person's spiritual dimension, so it is understandable that various religions have formed and become factional.

The Bible, Buddhist writings, and other scriptures all were written by human's relative evaluation and speculation in each era. However, there were many unfortunate histories existing. They were sometimes taken advantage of or used for religious domination in order to complete the "principle of dimensional domination" as a tool of desire to dominate people by Self-righteous interpretation.

For example, if 10 disciples evaluate one saint, each disciple makes relative evaluation according to each different personality formation history, so that there is hardly any truth or fact about the saint. All truth exists in the consciousness of each spiritual dimension so that the cause of the evaluation and the basis in the subjectivity are based on the one's personality formation history and has nothing to do with another's or phenomenon.

Since people who live the way of PARAREVO understand that all causes and subjectivities are contained inside one's own consciousness, so that all phenomena are the result of projection of one's own consciousness. They accomplish Self-completion bearing Self-responsibility to accept all things as they are with gratitude and happiness, totally and unconditionally, because they are the result that became phenomenon by one's own cause, problem, and assignment.

Since the "rule of causality" of the body from ancestors, based on the theory of Buddhist retribution, or the Atonement theory of the cross of Jesus, do not overcome the range of shifting responsibility by victim consciousness, existing religions should withdraw from all activities and immediately evacuate in order not to drive the earth into destruction by religious struggles. They would fade away once the PARAREVO theory proved their incompetence.

Unless the common existing purpose and existing value for human beings manifest in this world, we will never reach the universal truth.

The PARAREVO theory distinguishes the purpose and the goal in life. The purpose is *to accomplish Self-completion to graduate from the earth star,* the prison planet, and the goal is *to accomplish Self-realization of individual art of each person.*

2-61. The earth star is filled with delusions and illusions by supposition and speculation

Since each person has different consciousness of individual mental entity based on totally different personality formation history, when one person tells one fact to ten people successively, a completely different content from the initial fact will be transmitted to the tenth person. A person who is full of love catches one fact focusing with love, and a person who is full of ONSHU catches the same fact focusing with ONSHU as the truth.

Different individual mental entity transforms with each feeling range, so it will change to totally different information, and even if ten people hear one fact at the same time, the way to catch and the way to interpret and evaluate will be different because each individual is the cause and the subject.

Based on the facts in religious scripts, which have been passed

Chapter Two ☆ The Deriving Point

down for thousands of years, when religious people and religious scholars in the present time discuss what the saints are, their personality based on the spiritual dimension of being spiritually evolved to the present, are a world apart from the saint era, and of course they never met the saints, so only delusion and illusion exist based on their Self-evaluation and supposition. No matter what historians and archaeologists feel, think, and evaluate regarding past history, no historical fact exists in their theory but only their speculation and own evaluation exist as delusion and illusion. The past history is produced by the concept of virtual world, an imaginary world, which the brain of each person creates. It is because there is the rule of the universe that the truth only exists in zero time as now, even if fact exists in the past.

Religious doctrines can be theorized in any way for the cults` own convenience. There is no fact to be reached even if psychics of the astral plane of a lower dimension talk about the spiritual world within the range of the physical domination. Moreover, if a psychic is not able to wrestle with his/her issues or problems based on the "rule of reincarnation," how they can persuade others.

Atomic physics in the natural science and the world of quantum theory are the same thing, and there is no fact yet that human beings have confirmed the solid model of a molecule. There is also no fact that they have confirmed the atom or electron. They never go beyond the bounds of speculation and supposition because theoretical and empirical formula happens to be consistent for the most part. Presently the scientific world still remains in the stage of atomic model and nobody can even confirm an original form of the atom. It is left to speculation and supposition, even the era of scientific almighty principle. Therefore, it is no exaggeration to say that we are living a life of delusion and illusion because all things, such as rumors and mass media reports, are speculation and supposition and even facts are not guaranteed.

For that reason, if our life is based on the "principle of dimensional integration" of love, the past should be integrated to the present day, and the present day should be integrated to the present moment. However, actually, we are dominated by the old religious doctrines, and it created the problems as the source of evil and made reality complicated. If men of religion who are ignorant of this justify the past religious doctrines and teach them in the present, it is nothing but the "principle of dimensional domination" by ONSHU, and if they discuss the past religious doctrines as facts and distort the truth of the present, the religions themselves become the source of extreme sin which confuses people.

2-62. Religion will become archaic and fade away

In the universe, whether there is religion or not, *the fact exists that we are alive by the presence of the spiritual consciousness entity based on SHINSEI, and we wear a physical body,* so we should have courage and persistence in our belief to carry us through for the undeniable existentialism.

To love means to understand, to understand means to reach to conviction, and conviction will be specialized to belief, and belief will give you courage and power for creation. Truth exists only in the consciousness based on SHINSEI, and is directed to each person's spiritual dimension. The lesson of truth is contained in

Chapter Two ☆ The Deriving Point

yourself, so you, the individual mental entity, are the religion itself. You are the *only one able to save yourself,* and we could not find any fact in our history that unreliable religious doctrines or ceremonies by fake religious leaders or phony mediums can save our souls.

This is because, according to the PARAREVO theory, *in order to guarantee the "rule of freedom," the principle of Self-responsibility is secured, so there is no salvation by another existence.* Since salvation for the spiritual consciousness entity is unconditionally and totally left to your Self-administration and Self-responsibility with your Self-determination it will be done only when you practice the way of PARAREVO and accomplish Self-completion.

I will explain this using Christianity for an example. The Cross of Jesus was a matter of Jesus himself. He directed the phenomenon to himself in order to save himself. On the Cross, Jesus said the famous words "Please forgive them." This was his big mistake and sin. Because Jesus could not transcend the ONSHU, he shifted the responsibility to others by separating himself outside (external separation) with victim consciousness. He should have done internal separation, which would separate his own internal consciousness between his "soul mind" and "body mind," and accepted it, unconditionally and totally, as it was with gratitude and happiness based on SHINSEI, and attained Self-completion by truth. That would put his spiritual evolution in a higher spiritual dimension. External separation is a behavior that blames others for everything, according to the theory of right and wrong based on external evaluation, and as a result, you are falling into victim consciousness saying this person is bad, it is that person's responsibility, or it is a sin by those people, and directing your consciousness by shifting responsibility to others.

If religions had accomplished the principle of Self-responsibility by the "cosmological evidence" based on the PARAREVO theory, the theory of physical causality that is reactionary retribution to direct the cause to the past, as the theory of original sin or guilt of ancestors, that consider victim consciousness by the physical domination and shifting responsibility as supremacy, would be gone and not exist on the earth star. And, if it had been done, we would have been released from *the "principle of dependence and domination,"* and victims of religious dependence would have vanished, and we could have directed to Self-Enlightenment and spiritual evolution by *the "principle of independence and freedom."*

Therefore, if you believe the archaic Bible, Buddhist writings or other scriptures as fact and live your life by them, your spiritual consciousness entity is dominated by the past and you will live by being at the mercy of delusions and illusions in temporal life. Over time, religions will become archaic, and the spiritual civilization will be left out by the material civilization and inevitably loose integrity, so that we will face a time of destruction of the earth itself by *the threat of nuclear weapons* in the material civilization.

2-63. Sexual desire cannot be released by religion

In the future, due to scientific civilization, various information will become mixed up, confused, and overflow in disorder to induce undifferentiated sexual desire in youth and stimulate poor sexual impulse, and along with them, sexual crimes, and violent crimes will occur frequently. When we see that information, such as child

Chapter Two ☆ The Deriving Point

pornography, is sent through mass media and/or Internet, we could say that old-fashioned ideas of religions doctrines and ethics about sex has lost the power to control sexual desire consciousness and becomes inadequate.

It is because instinct transcends reason, so the sexual desire consciousness, one of the instinctive survival consciousnesses, has been transformed into domination desire and ultimately becomes demand and desire by violent domination. It is also confirmed as a fact, that right after a youth commits a violent crime by undifferentiated sexual impulse, he has a tendency to masturbate. Sexual impulse and violent impulse co-exist as the relative instinctive desire consciousness.

For instance, some religious nations openly discriminate against women by legalizing polygamy, which often co-exists with violence, and it makes a situation which extremely delays spiritual evolution. Those two connoted desires create the relative original power at the relative dimensions, and always have potential to activate the consciousness of sexual domination synergistically. By misperception of sex and the chaotic flood of sex education and information, the undeveloped youth brain, the core of sexual desire, is stimulated and makes escalating sexual fantasies and illusions, then brings on undifferentiated sexual impulses. In order to embody the fantasy and illusion of undifferentiated sexual desire, they will evoke undifferentiated sexual impulse to seek substantial stimulation, and drive impulse sensation to violent domination, so it would be likely that they will abuse their wife and children.

As long as we continue to shoulder the "instinctive survival consciousnesses" as fate, it will be impossible to transcend the "instinctive remaining consciousness" and dispel sexual corruption, sexual crimes, delinquency and violent crimes, from the world. Since the first creature was born on the earth star, terrestrial life has accomplished evolution by differentiating into various living things through 3.8 billion years. In order to sustain life with the physical body in the environment of the prison star, terrestrial life equally shoulders the fate to continue to survive by connoting the two largest desires, the dietary desire consciousness and the sexual desire consciousness, as the "instinctive survival consciousnesses."

When we look at the process of the evolution of human beings from bacteria, primitive life entity, to Homo sapiens, intelligent life entity, it started from a very simple structure, the relative structure of amino acids and DNA, and gradually became differentiated by starting cell division from one-celled bacteria through viruses and ameba. The original bacteria and initial organisms had not yet made the sexual differentiation of "negative and positive," so they were asexual. They evolved from non-acidophilus bacteria, which disliked acid, to acidophilus bacteria which preferred acid, "cyan bacteria," and succeeded in creating enormous energy by gradually accomplishing the environmental adaptation accompanied with the change in the global environment. This accomplishment was an epoch-making evolution.

It started from an extremely simple asexual entity to a gradual differentiation of "negative and positive," and through evolution, accomplished sexual differentiation, like stamens and pistils for plants and female and male for animals. Especially in animals, the sexual differentiation was accomplished remarkably, so that each role and responsibility was separated clearly and functioned as a

Chapter Two ☆ The Deriving Point

sexually separated life entity.

The role and responsibility to the "instinctive survival consciousnesses" was divided by sexual differentiation, so that the male has been responsible for the dominating structure of dietary desire consciousness and the female has been responsible for the preservation of species of the sexual desire consciousness and inheritance of genetic information.

Through the evolution processes, the most concretely appearing phenomenon is distinguishability and release of the sexual desire consciousness in sexual relationship based on sexual differentiation.

As I explained before, the "soul mind" is the intention to be directed by the love of spiritual consciousness entity, and the "body mind" is the intention to be directed by the desire of the physical body. "Soul mind" is the manifestation of consciousness and motive based on the love of "logos," and "body mind" is the manifestation of consciousness and motive based on the desire of "Eros." "Logos" is the virtue of selflessness based on the love for others, and "Eros" is the vice of desire based on egoism and narcissism. Also, "Logos" is the "logical nature" based on love in accordance with the rule of the universe, and "Eros" is the "illogical nature" based on desire in accordance with the rule of the earth. The love of "Logos" is the true nature based on love, and is the qualitative grace which each person has. Both negative and positive, and male and female exist in each person and all elements form the nature of the person.

The lower living things have the least sexual differentiation. The spiritual evolution has been achieved more by the middle to the higher-animals, and they have changed shape and form remarkably, to the sexual separated life entity accompanied with sexual differentiation.

In the major trend of the evolutional process of human beings, there is a hypothesis that evolution has been done from ape-man (Australopithecus) to hominid (Homo erectus), and next to the ancient people (Homo Neanderthal man) and then to new people (Homo sapiens). "Homo" mean people who do something. Homo erectus means biped people and Homo sapiens means people use wisdom.

The theory of PARAREVO is not to discuss anthropology, but the most important meaning and significance is to consider verifying and clarifying the mechanism and system cosmologically, that is, what kind of driving force directed the spiritual evolution and the physical evolution.

The crucial difference in ecological behavior between general animals and apes, such as the long-armed ape, orangutans, gorillas, chimpanzees, and chimpanzee bonobos, is the physiological behavior pattern in sexual relations. General animals do not engage in sexual relations unless it is in a breeding season. On the other hand, apes demonstrate superiority and dominance by sexual relations or as a means of communication, so they form harmony and order by determining the social group ranking.

It was about 600 million years ago that the ancestors of human beings differentiated and evolved to chimpanzee bonobos, and then about 16 million years ago, they achieved major evolution to Homo sapiens. The significant evolution to human beings was to act in a biped manner, to start using tools skillfully together with the development of the brain, and to start using complex languages, wearing clothes, and using fire.

Chapter Two ☆ The Deriving Point

As stated in the Old Testament, Adam and Eve, who had no shame in being naked, covered the their genitals with fig leaves after obtaining the wisdom to know the difference between right and wrong, and begin avoiding lustful sexual relations and feel shame and separation toward sexuality, so the civilization and culture achieved rapid evolution, and opened the door for the evolution toward higher organisms. This would prove that by releasing the sexual desire consciousness, one of the instinctive survival consciousnesses, we had come on the road of spiritual evolution reliably.

Although the theoretic interpretation of the Bible preaches that the original sin was that Adam and Eve were seduced by the snake and ate the fruit of good and evil, breaking the commandments of God.

Non-PAREVO theory makes out that the act to cover the genitals with fig leaves in order to hide the sin of sexual corruption proves immorality, and the act itself is the original sin. However, the theory of PAREVO teaches the evolutional process of human beings by the totally opposite interpretation. It says that high differentiation of sexual ethics is the driving force of evolution, so that covering the genitals as protection from sexual corruption is the result of dimensional integration by sexual differentiation. If it is the original sin, the sexual relations, like chimpanzee bonobo being naked, are still justified as a social order and continuously pass on sexual corruption. In fact, the naked tribes, who inhabit the interior of Africa or the Amazon, do not engage in a civilized and cultural life at the present time.

Let's consider that evolution is a precondition of our history.

I think that when the sexual differentiation from ape to higher dimension was accomplished, and the trial to control sexual relations by covering the genitals, the symbol of sexual desire consciousness, achieved evolution to a higher spiritual dimension by directing the spiritual evolution. So, releasing the sexual desire consciousness, is the driving force and the fundamental equation to direct the personality transformation and the spiritual evolution to a higher spiritual dimension from Homo sapiens to Homo philosophical and then to Homo cosmology (cosmological life entity). In order for human beings to achieve the spiritual evolution, we must evolve from *"undifferentiated sexual desire consciousness"* to *"mid-differentiated sexual separated consciousness,"* and furthermore, must achieve new *regeneration of SHINSEI and soul to "SHINSEI integrated life entity"* with spiritual evolution to a high differentiated sexual integrated consciousness. Otherwise we will never be released, eternally, from the prison star.

2-64. The 21st century plunges into the era of ending the prison star

When the material civilization greatly transcends the spiritual civilization, losing the integration completely, undifferentiated sexual impulse and unrestricted violent impulse are united and become out of control, and the world of sexual corruption manifests, such as in the cities of Sodom and Gomorrah. Then, the end of human history will be coming.

If religious conflicts and personality destructions come at the same time, and the material civilization such as nuclear bombs and

Chapter Two ☆ The Deriving Point

chemical weapons are used for horrible terrorism, it could cause the end of the world.

People who have lack of love syndrome, are underdeveloped, mentally immature, and dependent, because they are dominated by the wrong rule of causality between parents and children, potentially, invoke undifferentiated sexual impulse and destructive violent impulse at the same time, so that someday, the earth star will be destructed, like in a video game, by those same people.

The material civilization has already developed atomic bombs and hydrogen bombs, and spread them all over the world. Because of their enormous power, it will be destroying hundreds of earth stars. It is no exaggeration to say that the material civilization has already reached the time of the decline, or termination, of the religious age.

We desperately need the emergence of a new mental civilization, which can drastically reform theoretical frameworks and values of the existing religions and philosophy, and direct us to the opposite, which will secure the future of the earth.

Now is the time to complete the spiritual and mental paradigm revolution in which each person embraces Self-contained SHINSEI by new cosmological truth called *the PARAREVO theory,* which is based on the "cosmological evidence." And everybody in the world should integrate and unite good individuality with SHINSEI, as the common denominator, to accomplish Self-completion in dimensional integration by directing the spiritual consciousness entity to the universe.

We must establish global collaboration with each person's sentiment world and individual personality dimension. The 20th century was a period of ideological struggle between communism and capitalism. The 21st century is the time to build a new spiritual civilization that can surpass the material civilization. In order to do so, we must have the courage to release the old mental cultures and build a new mental culture.

Now, the earth star is asked by the universe whether it will choose the path to destruction by religious wars and religious terrorism with the background of monotheism, or choose the path to evolution and creation by directing to the way of life of PARAREVO by the PARAREVO theory.

2-65. Crisis can be avoided by liberation from religious curse

Because religions have the possibility to transcend reason and the verge of life and death, and make people turn to fanatical actions such as terrorism, it could be said that the end of human beings is left to religious wars and religious terrorism. The ideological stage, such as communism and capitalism, is only centered in physical world benefits by worldly principle based on material and physical values, so Self-control powers the functions to live in this world.

However, some religions are practicing brainwashing education from infancy with lies and untrue theories and values, and incite youth to unquestioning belief and fanaticism to make them go to riots or force them to suicide bombing, so the earth star contains the danger to collapse in the extension of those incidents. In the monotheistic view of God, based on the "earth logical evidence," God is the absolute, one and only creator, so there is a clear sense of

Chapter Two ☆ The Deriving Point

separation between God and the whole creation world.

On the other hand, SHINSEI of the universe, based on the "cosmological evidence," is the source of power of sustainable freedom and love which keeps expanding eternally and limitlessly from the minimum to the maximum of the world. It is contained in all things existing in the entire universe, and all things exist in each spiritual dimension freely and equally, based on the "rule of the relative wave and the relative original power." SHINSEI and the universe are the relative presence which derived simultaneously and synchronically based on the "rule of entropy relativity," and they generate and develop for directing to the spiritual dimension of a higher rank, by the "principle of dimensional integration and the relative original power," which is sustainable and is derived in the slight fluctuation of imperfection between SHINSEI, the relative subject, and the whole creation world in the entire universe, the relative object, and make it possible to exist eternally.

If the universe exists based on perfection without fluctuation, it won't generate and develop, so it will be restrained and there will be no occurrence of or exchange in energy. The existence of SHINSEI itself is no exception. It creates a sustainable system for eternal evolution for subjective love and objective happiness by opening the path of feeling to a higher rank by relative original power generated between love and happiness based on the "principle of dimensional integration."

SHINSEI is not the absolute or only presence but the relative one. *There is nothing absolute existing in the universe.* However, the monotheism belief is that only one God exists and it is an absolute presence, so by creating that God it requires a perfect person like

Jesus, and religiously creates the polarization of good and evil, and it has conveniently used the pyramid type dominating structure for legalization. *Since all religions do not reach to the truth, they are not able to direct the truth to one purpose, which is to graduate from the earth star.*

This evidence proves that religions create the pyramid type dominating structure systematically for the prison star, and then an autocratic leader appears, making the absolute God. So, it is Self-righteous and exclusive to other religions by making the absolute religious doctrines. All religions are Self-righteous and exclusive and have done specific brainwashing to display the presence of their religious group. In particular, monotheistic religions have a tendency to be extremely Self-righteous and exclusive. The logic of monotheism believes that the God, which their ancestors decided, is the one and only and absolute presence.

It will never happen that religions will admit relative presence for co-existence, mutual prosperity, and symbiosis for human beings to direct the world of collaboration. That is the reason conflicts and wars for territory and religious problems are endless. Always there is the theory of the original sin, the theory of corruption, and the theory of good and evil in the center, and by insisting the fundamentalism, and always dividing two opposite things such as good or evil, or right or wrong, and searching for the point of confrontation, they try to justify and insist on their goodness.

Since accepting other Gods and religions is an act of disloyalty equal to religious corruption, they wield their principles such as Islamic fundamentalism and Christian fundamentalism, because of their lack of forgiveness, tolerance, and acceptance. In fact, they

Chapter Two ☆ The Deriving Point

easily become a hot bed for cult religions and produce unquestioning believers and fanatics to the world by Self-righteous interpretation of religious doctrines, and have exposed the fragility and dangers of monotheism.

However, originally, religion problems and territorial problems were not about problems of religions or ethnics.

Although they talk about God and religion, the fundamental cause for the conflicts are instinctive desires called the domination desire and material desire based on the instinctive survival consciousnesses, which the destiny for the terrestrial life from the beginning and source of power but nothing else, because *the "original sin consciousness" is in "original existing consciousnesses."* Even though they substitute the physical desire to religious theory and rehash it, it is impossible to surpass and transcend the "instinctive survival consciousnesses."

There are also territorial disputes in the animal world. It is an act of instinct that dogs do marking like conditioned reflex, when they go for walk. Similarly, since human beings are also terrestrial life, that desire and persistence in territory and land are our fate as instinct. Religious groups are supposed to respect in spirit; however, they are still trapped by material tangible things. Pompous and huge buildings and museums have been built in various places as symbols of power and they are left all over the world as the fingerprints of undeniable fact.

2-66. Religious struggles are the common crisis of the earth star

Religions have tied the minds of people with lies and untrue doctrines, which are the root of all evil in the earth star, by hiding the physical desire instincts, the instinctive survival consciousnesses, by legalizing the "principle of dimensional domination," the accepted opinion in the prison star, and by playing a role and responsibility, as *the "guard of the prison star."*

If an extremist leader takes a stand against a fanatical leader of monotheism when that leader obtains a nuclear bomb, human beings will probably draw the worst scenario in the future. If Islam, which is the largest religion in the world, and Christianity, which has the background of Judaism, become united by integrating ONSHU with love, according to the PARAREVO theory, it will be the happiest thing for the earth star.

It is because, religions existing now as Judaism, Christianity, and Islam, spread out all over the world as the descendants of Abraham, are by the triangle system of the legal wife of Abraham, Sarah, her biological child, Isaac, and the concubine Hagar, with illegitimate child, Ishmael, 4000 years ago. So if sorrow and ONSHU, the spiritual core of ONSHU, are not to be released and advance further, again human beings will draw the worst scenario.

So, I will give my analysis of the Old Testament, from the viewpoint of the principal of the universe, in the next few paragraphs. It won't be necessary to check word for word, but I will point out several contradictions and explain those according to the PARAREVO theory.

Chapter Two ☆ The Deriving Point

2-67. The Old Testament is the genealogy of genetic linkage from Eve

I will explain in detail about the main causes and circumstances which Judaism and Islam became involved in a family quarrel by reading the *"rule of sorrow and ONSHU in the triangle relationship"* based on the "earth logical evidence."

In the first chapter, the first section of Matthew in the New Testament, it starts as "the generation of Jesus Christ, the son of David, the son of Abraham." In the sixteenth section, it says that "Jacob was the father of Joseph who was the husband of Mary." If Jesus Christ was truly born by Mary's virgin birth, he should not have had any relationship in the bloodline with Joseph. So the exact description should be the genealogy of Joseph, the husband of Mary, instead of the one of Jesus. In other words, there is a misconception and false information from the first to the sixteenth section, in the first chapter of Matthew in the New Testament.

Since the Bible is written, from start to finish, about the chain of genetic code called the family tree with the "rule of physical causality" based on the rule of "body is subjective and spirit is objective," it is equal to the "rule of retribution" in Buddhism. It does not transcend the category of the instinctive survival consciousnesses. We should presuppose the Bible in this way. Otherwise, we are at the mercy of delusions and illusions of the Bible, and directed to wrong interpretations. As a result, hundreds of thousands of new religions have emerged from one book, the Bible.

The Old Testament is the genealogy book, starting from Adam and Eve, written about the incidents that happened in marital and parent-child relationships and families, which were developed as family stories in each era. So, the Bible is just a book in which is written pedigree facts surrounding kinship as stories, according to the "rule of the genetic chain" by the "rule of physical causality" based on the rule of "body is subjective and spirit is objective." But, I could say that the Bible is the mighty works of logos (languages) and has preserved this long family tree as a book.

The family tree started with Adam and Eve, and Cain, the first-born son, Abel, the second son and Seth, the third son. Cain killed Abel, and the Old Testament began from the genealogy of Seth. Noah, of Noah`s Ark, was born as the tenth generation from Seth. The saint Abraham was born as the 21st generation from Adam, and was the tenth generation from Shem, the son of Noah.

The Old Testament has been written with facts which happened in the representative families, tribes, and ethnic groups in each era according to the "rule of the genetic chain" based on the "rule of physical causality," and still has not transcended the instinctive survival consciousnesses, which means it is a history book of lustful sexual misconducts, with struggles, massacre, and love plunder, which is far from the book called the Bible.

Clarifying the equation of the nature of humanity is easily verified and proven, in accordance with the PARAREVO theory, by untying the dominating desire by the sexual desire consciousness, and the material desire by the dietary desire consciousness, based on the instinctive survival consciousnesses. The equation for *the core of ONSHU,* inherited to lineage, is easy to understand. It manifests by the instinctive remaining consciousness, inherited in lineage, which created the love and hatred of women by *the triangle relationship between husband, wife, and mistress* and made the core

Chapter Two ☆ The Deriving Point

of ONSHU, since the "rule of the genetic chain" is written in the genetic code of women's mitochondria only.

According to a medieval text, known as *The Alphabet of Ben Sira* (8th~10th century), Adam had a wife whose name was Lilith before he married Eve. She requested superiority over Adam for the sex position. But, Adam argued that man should be superior because he wanted to place Lilith under his domination. I believe Lilith understood that women were the relative subjectivity. This is supported by the fact that men have nipples even though they do not need them as a function of the male body. So, I could say that women were the body model in the beginning. In the quarrel with Adam, Lilith responded as follows. "We are equal to each other inasmuch as we were both created from the earth," but he tried to suppress her with his power. Lilith is described as a demon in many writings. It was because the male domination structure on the earth had to be justified and legalized dominantly. So the name of Lilith was not mentioned in the Old Testament intentionally, instead she was referred to as some kind of demon. If Adam had humbly served Lilith at that time, human beings would have evolved more at that point.

Also, Cain was not a child of Eve, but was a son from Lilith when Adam impregnated Lilith by force. The real reason Cain murdered Abel, was discord and ONSHU between half-brothers with the same father.

Next, I would like to describe the core of ONSHU, why Judaism and Islam have family discord.

★See diagram "Family Tree of Earth Bible based on the Physical Causality" on P154, P155

2-68. The core of ONSHU of Judaism and Islam

Judaism and Islam are understood as completely different religions, but actually, the two religions have the same root. The God named Yahweh that the Jewish believe in, and the God named Allah that Muslims believe in, are the same God, and they only differ in language, Hebrew for Jewish and Arabic for Islam. Islam and Christianity are the parent-child religions born from Judaism, and even though Christianity and Islam are the brotherly religions, the difference is the brotherly relationship of ONSHU between legitimate child and illegitimate child.

The reason these two religions of half-siblings from different mothers with the same root have such family discord, is because the spark of ONSHU was ignited by sorrow and ONSHU in the triangle relationship which began in the family four thousand years ago. Believers in Judaism, Christianity, and Islam all respected a person called Abraham and worshiped him as a Saint. He is called "the Father of Faith," and all believers of those three religions are considered "the ancestors of Abraham."

Abraham was the leader of a nomadic tribe who journeyed with his people. One day, because his people were suffering from hunger, he had to stop in Egypt, the land of the gentile. Abraham had a beautiful wife named Sarai. Out of fear for his own life, he asked her to pretend that they were siblings. This was because he thought the Pharaoh, the king of Egypt, might want to possess her at first sight because of her beauty, and probably have him killed. However, if they were siblings, his life would be spared. Abraham even tried to give the Pharaoh his wife's chastity, while pleading for his life.

Chapter Two ☆ The Deriving Point

Family Tree of Earth Bible based on the physical causality

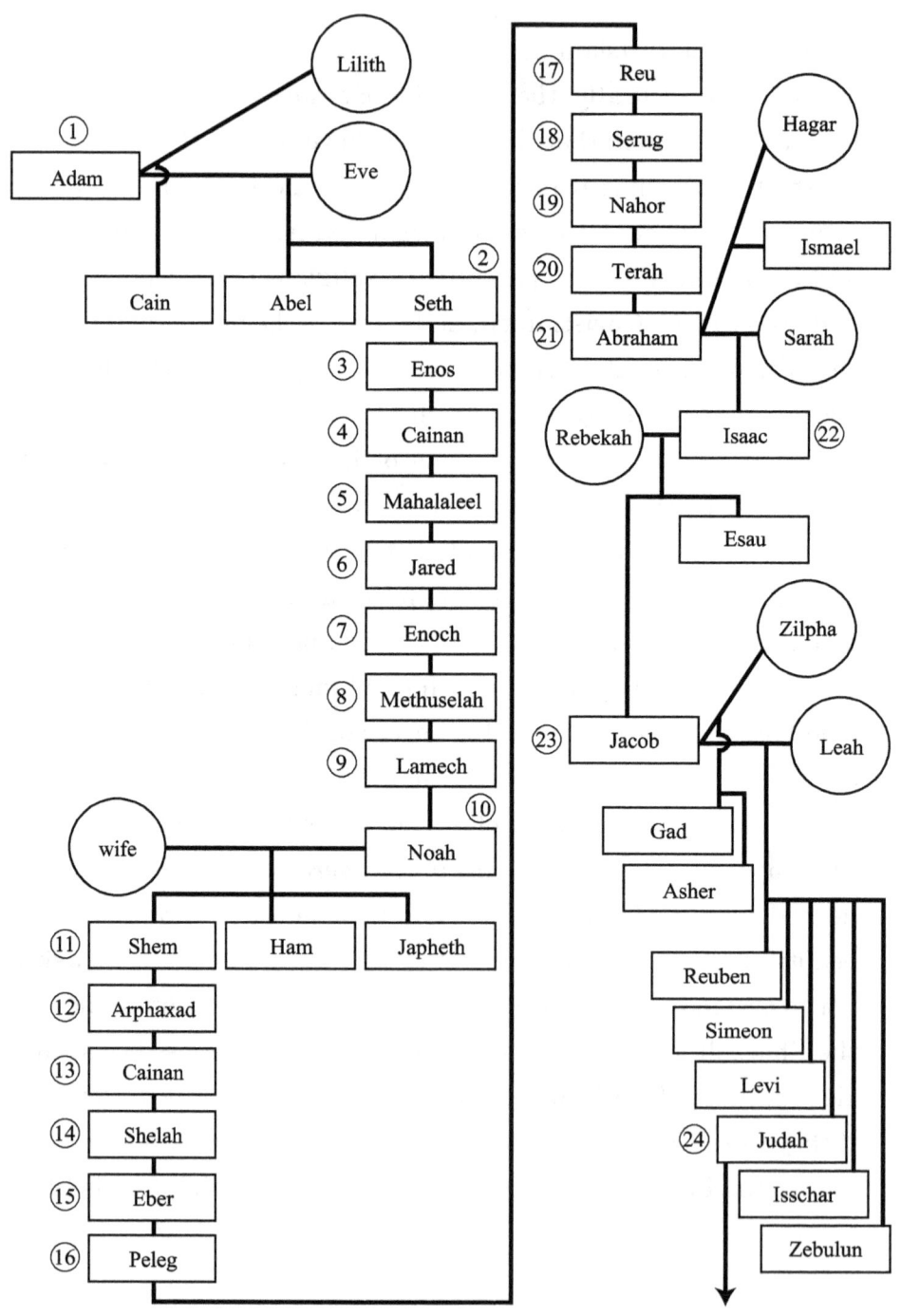

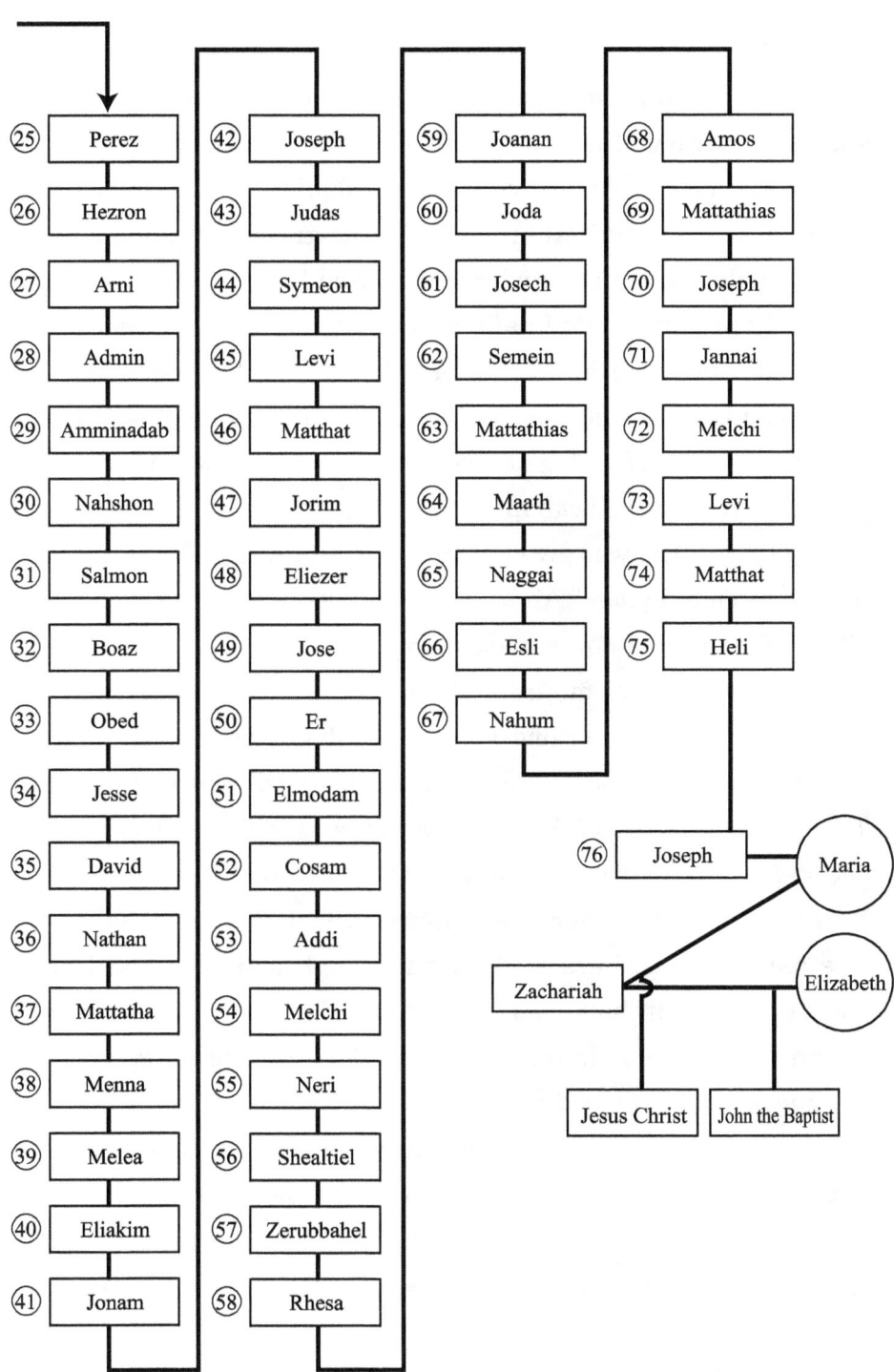

Chapter Two ☆ The Deriving Point

Now I would like to explain this incident from her point of view. Sarai wanted to protect her chastity and love to her husband, so she risked her own life by allowing herself to become exposed to the plague. Because of her devotion to her husband, the Pharaoh forgave Abraham's lie, and Abraham's family was given food, supplies and slaves, male and female, and released from Egypt.

The Abraham family finally arrived in the land of Canaan and they had a peaceful life. However, Abraham and Sarai had a big heartache because they had no child. Sarai anguished over being barren, so she made a big decision because she wanted to preserve the blood lineage of Abraham. She said to Abraham, "I have a maid named Hagar who was given to me by the Pharaoh in Egypt. Please have your child by her." Abraham did exactly what she asked. Soon Hagar conceived a boy named Ishmael. The maid Hagar became condescending to her mistress, Sarai.

After that, an angel came down to Abraham and said, "Abraham, change Sarai's name to Sara. Soon Sara will conceive a child. Then name him Isaac." When Abraham was told this, he chuckled because he and Sara were both old and Sara had already finished her menopause. However, she conceived and gave a birth. The child was named Isaac. Sara could not forgive Hagar who had looked down on her even though she was her maid, so she asked Abraham to banish Hagar and Ishmael to the wilderness. Abraham accepted her appeal and banished them.

Hagar and Ishmael ran out of water and food in the wilderness, but an angel came in the dust storms when they were nearly dead. Hager was told that "thy son Ishmael will make a great nation for his people." Then, the dust storm was gone and a well appeared before Hagar and Ishmael, so they survived.

Later, the angel appeared to Abraham and said, "Offer thy son Isaac as sacrifice." Abraham reached the summit of Mount Moriah after three days and three nights of suffering and struggling, to sacrifice Isaac, his only son with Sara. Abraham decided to sacrifice Isaac to return him to God when God asked, because he was given by God. When Abraham was about to turn the knife blade and fire on Isaac, God said "Oh, Abraham, now I know thou are the one to be afraid of thy God. Thou should not kill thy son, Isaac." Just then a ram in the brush got caught in a thorn bush, so he sacrificed it instead. This is a brief summary about the incidents which happened in Abraham's family.

2-69. The "rule of sorrow and ONSHU in the triangle relationship" that happened in Abraham's family

The facts that happened in Abraham's family superbly manifest the condensation of two rules, one based on the "earth logical evidence" and the other based on the "cosmological evidence." Let's analyze how each rule was developed, based on the PARAREVO theory.

First of all, there were the incidents when Abraham stayed temporarily in Egypt. It was a corrupt mistake of selfish egotism in Abraham's male type dominating structure toward women when he tried to give his wife's chastity away in exchange for his own life, based on the "earth logical evidence." We can understand this incident from the view of Sarah's devoted mental world based on the "cosmological evidence." She completed herself with love by her

Chapter Two ☆ The Deriving Point

own Self-determination and Self-responsibility to preserve her own chastity and love and loyalty to her husband, even though she was exposed to an epidemic which put her life at risk.

Sarah`s *great virtues of unselfishness by Self-sacrifice* protected her family enabling them to receive a log of tribute and servants from the Pharaoh. Also, she made Self-determination to protect the lineage of Abraham, so she took the full responsibility to the lineage even though she gave her husband to her own maidservant, and completed herself by Self-responsibility. Because of her selflessness, she received a child to her womb from the spiritual world by surpassing and transcending the ONSHU of Hagar and Ishmael with love.

However, she made a big mistake, based on the "earth logical evidence." When Sarah received Isaac, she should have loved the illegitimate child, Ishmael, more than her real child, which means that she needed a strong commitment to be humble by directing to the "soul mind," the relative subject, according to the "principle of dimensional integration" by internal separation, and must have sentiment with humble love toward Hagar and feel that she is serving obediently. But, Sarah lost out to her own evil. She asked Abraham to banish Hagar and Ishmael to the wilderness with the emotion of ONSHU according to the "principle of dimensional domination" by external separation, and it infuriated the heavens above. This ordeal was the test called the consecration of Isaac, in which she had to put her own biological child for sacrifice. Consequently, one of the universal rules of "the exclusive theory of jealousy" supports the proof *to sacrifice the most loving thing by expelling ONSHU.*

The sacrifice of Isaac was avoided by the faith of Abraham. This is the reason that Abraham's Self-sacrificing faith to God, offering his own child when God asked, had been idealized and is still praised by Judaism, Islam, and Christianity, and he was respected as "the Father of Faith" and worshiped as a saint. However, it is also a fact that this symbolized and idealized faith is used for the holy war called Jihad and is a hotbed for suicide-bomb type of terrorism.

Between Sarah and Abraham, which had more attachment to Isaac? By verifying the circumstances, until old Sarah gave birth to Isaac, she surpassed and transcended all trials and ONSHU by love, and finally received her precious child from the spiritual world after feeling like tearing herself to pieces. Was it easy to accept and say yes when she was asked by God to sacrifice her precious son? Perhaps Sarah had far more attachment to Isaac than did Abraham. Since Sarah was a spiritually wise woman, she probably realized intuitively that expelling Hagar and Ishmael infringed on the rule of the universe. Sarah must have realized her own stupidity and poor judgment, and repented from her heart, and made Self-determination to accept all things humbly, sincerely, unconditionally and fully, and made Self-completion by transcending "body mind" with "soul mind" by surpassing all sorrow and ONSHU.

So, since Sarah made Self-completion with the mental victory of love, Abraham could become the victor of the faith. The victory of the faith of Abraham could not be completed without Sarah's victory of transcendent love. Therefore, behind the Self-actualization in the substantial success of man, there is a Self-completion of victory of mental love of woman, so that it is proof that the key for all fortunes is in the hands of women who contain the logic of love, integration, and creation, inside.

Chapter Two ☆ The Deriving Point

However, Sarah depicted the worst-case scenario by exiling Hagar and Ishmael into the wilderness, and superscripted the historical ONSHU. This woman's mistake of love built the world of ONSHU for 4,000 continuous years, and became the main cause for Jewish and Muslim to continue the hostile structure. Hagar and Ishmael burned strong sorrow and ONSHU into their minds against Sarah and Isaac, and their descendants inherited the hatred and grudge toward Abraham's family and lineage throughout history, directing the spiritual feeling of resentment by victim consciousness and shifting responsibility to the outside, dominating "soul mind" by "body mind", according to the "principle of dimensional domination" by external separation.

A feud and ONSHU between Abraham's lawful wife Sarah and concubine Hagar, and a feud and ONSHU between legitimate son Isaac and illegitimate son Ishmael, in Abraham's family, continued throughout history because of "inveterate grudge and genes of women."

"Isaac people" who had the lineage of Sarah, generated Jesus who was called Messiah by Judaism, and spread their belief over the world, as Christianity. "Ishmael people" who had the lineage of Hagar and inherited the blood of Egyptians, generated the prophet Muhammad through the lineage of Arabs, and spread their belief as the religion called Islam, which had the largest number of followers in the world, and built a gigantic group of descendants of Abraham, more than 40 million in the world today. By *the "rule of exclusive theory of jealousy,"* "Arab people" who are descendants of the "Ishmael people" exiled to the wilderness by Sarah, remain in the Middle East, and the Jewish people who are descendants of the

"Isaac people" who exiled Hagar and Ishmael to the wilderness, lost their nation and became the people of wander in the world.

Until the nation of Israel was established in 1948 by the Zionist movement centered by Ben-Gurion, after World War II, Jewish people had been expelled and spread out around the world, especially in Europe, as the wandering people without a country. However, ONSHU has not been released yet, even though 4,000 years have passed, and by repeating the history of conflict and destruction, it will eventually face the history of the final chapter.

2-70. Great virtues of unselfishness by Self-sacrifice

The "rule of sorrow and ONSHU in the triangle relationship" which happened in Abraham's family, is the epitome of all rules, mechanisms, and systems in the prison star, based on the "earth logical evidence." This "rule of sorrow and ONSHU in the triangle relationship" between Abraham, his lawful wife Sarah and his concubine Hagar formed discord and ONSHU between legitimate child Isaac and illegitimate child Ishmael, and came down through history with ONSHU and DNA of women, then expanded from the Abraham family to clans, ethnic groups and nations. This is the fateful rule of ONSHU that human beings must overcome and surpass by human love on the earth star.

The equation of cosmological love is stepping up the spiritual dimension by overcoming and surpassing ONSHU by love, based on the PARAREVO theory *that releasing one's own ONSHU by loving ONSHU itself,* accomplishes Self-completion of the personality transformation and spiritual dimension according to the "principle

Chapter Two ☆ The Deriving Point

of dimensional integration" by internal separation, with full and unconditional acceptance of external conditions.

For example, Hagar was a foreigner and maidservant, so to Sarah who came from the proud Jewish nation, Hagar was a low rank, contemptible existence. When Sarah gave her beloved husband to Hager, it meant that she gave the best love to her ONSHU, so she would accomplish Self-completion of her sentiment world and personality dimension by overcoming and transcending her own status by love. Certainly, by providing love to an illegitimate child, she released her own firmly closed womb and was able to conceive her own child.

Envy is written in Japanese Kanji characters, as "woman and stone" and it surely seems to express the jealousy of a woman who is not able to produce children, since a barren woman is called UMAZUME (stone woman) in Japanese.

The important lesson, based on the PARAREVO theory, is that the infertile woman Sarah had overcome anguish and conflict toward the foreign woman Hagar in order to conceive a life from the spiritual world, and opened her own spiritual passage for conception. When Sarah let Hager receive her husband`s sperm by making Hagar`s womb open, based on the rule of "spirit is subjective and body is objective" by the "principle of dimensional integration" with internal separation, she released her own ONSHU by loving her ONSHU. Sarah then derived and prepared the spiritual consciousness entity of the spiritual dimension that is relative to her feeling, according to the "rule of relative original power" with the mind and spirit in the spiritual world. This rule explains that things will become phenomenon when the mind, which is the personality entity existing in this world, will be relative with the soul, which is the spiritual entity existing in the spiritual world, by opening the spiritual passage and connecting the relative wave to each other, and create the relative original power between them.

Saints and the righteous people were born to this world based on this rule. However, they did not become as they were by themselves, but were the fruition of love of great mothers. That was the cause and the subjectivity in the sentiment world and the spiritual dimension of mothers who hoped for conception by love, but not lewd sexual relations with undifferentiated sexual desire consciousness. The mental fluctuation between love and sexual desire was not perfect sexual separation, but better than undifferentiated sexual desire.

The intentions for conceptual relationship, to prepare in order to receive their souls according to the "rule of relative original power" with the mind and spirit, have important meaning and significance in the sentiment world and the spiritual dimension of Mary, the mother of Jesus, and Maya, the mother of Buddha. This is because *only women are given the function and authority for physical evolution and spiritual evolution from the universe.*

Man's role is to plant the seeds of sperm by undifferentiated sexual desire consciousness, and they became a catalyst for fertilization of egg. Besides, the egg has superiority in inheritance for physical genetic information. Mitochondria in the cells are only inherited from the mother's side, and when analyzing the DNA of mitochondria, it is possible to study all evolutional processes by tracing and analyzing the system of the mother's ancestors, and to elucidate the systematic distribution and the spread of the evolution between apes and humans. In fact, the difference in the size of eggs and sperm is very obvious. Since eggs are much bigger, it means that by the genetic code of women, the information about lineage and inheritance rights has been mostly dominated by the negative type superiority. Moreover, it is not too much to say that all things are in complete control by women, such as conception of a soul, lineage inheritance rights, and genetic recombination.

The soul of a good person and the soul of an evil person, and the physical desire consciousness, have been created and delivered by the sentiment world and the spiritual dimension of either love or ONSHU of women. The soul, which became relative and matched with the genetic information of a woman, is only able to descend by conception.

The core of historical evolution is directed by the sentiment world and spiritual dimension of women. The dimension of the soul and the structural arrangement of the physical genetic code of human beings, who will be delivered to this world, are determined by women. So it is no exaggeration to say that the future of the nation and the future of the world are left in the hands of women.

It is very important for our future how fast we can produce the spiritually wise and excellent women to this world. In reverse, we might reach the destruction of families, societies, ethnic groups, nations and the world by ignorant women who unquestioningly follow the male type dominating structure.

Frameworks of religious theories and values up to the 20th century will collapse and be reformed in the 21st century by spiritually wise women. Spiritually wise women and intelligently wise women are fundamentally different. Spiritually wise women are women who can produce *great virtues of unselfishness by Self-sacrifice* based on the spiritual world benefits, and intelligently wise women have a tendency to produce the *immorality of selfishness by the hypocrisy of Self-satisfaction* based on the physical world benefits.

In the world, several countries still legalize polygamy. This is because of either how women have become passive under the male type dominating structure and depend on it, or the religious doctrines have big defects and problems. Political power and male domination can't solve this problem. It would only lead to conflict and destruction and make the unfortunate chain expand by a negative spiral. However, when many spiritually wise women are produced in the societies of polygamy and caste system, religious doctrines will collapse naturally and the social systems will be reformed.

For the evolutionary history, women have integrated and created the causal negative invisible spiritual world, and men have dominated and reigned over the resultant positive real world, as the surface, and relatively, the sentiment world and the spiritual dimension of women have directed the evolution and constructed the history.

The rule of the universe is mechanized to *great virtues of unselfishness by Self-sacrifice,* which makes impossible things possible, and all functions in the entire universe are directed to freedom and systematized. However, the rule of the earth is mechanized to the *immorality of selfishness by the hypocrisy of Self-satisfaction,* which makes possible things impossible, and the common consciousness and ecological behavior of terrestrial life are directed to inconvenience and systematized.

2-71. Analysis of personality formation history of Adolf Hitler

Adolf Hitler was born on April 20, 1889 as the third child of six brothers, between the father Alois who was a customs officer and the mother Klara, in a small town of Braunau located at the border between Austria and Germany. Hitler also had two half siblings, because Klara was the third wife of Alois. Half-brother Alois II left home at the age of 14 and passed away at the age of 73. Half-sister Angela passed away at the age of 66. Of his biological brothers and sisters, the eldest son died at the age of 2, the eldest daughter died at the age of 2, the second son died at the age of 0, and younger brother Edmund died at the age of 6. His younger sister Baura, his only surviving sibling died at the age of 64.

Now, I would like to discuss Hitler's biological history based on the book written by Hermann von Goldschmidt and published in 1917. He was the senior clerk to Baron Salomon Rothschild. This is not a history book. The purpose of this is to verify the person, Hitler, according to the PARAREVO theory. I would like to verify the motion of his consciousness inside his "depth mentality" based on the "rule of the relative original power," and the process of his motivation directed to ONSHU by analyzing his personal formation history and spiritual formation history.

Regarding Hitler's paternal lineage, his grandmother Maria Anna had been apprenticed as a housekeeper at the home of millionaire Salomon Rothschild who was born as the second son between the founder of Rothschild Meyer and Gutouru, and inherited the Austrian family fortune. The Rothschild families were Jewish millionaires in Europe, with the head of the family in

Frankfurt, Germany.

While Maria Anna was working at the Rothschild's, she became pregnant. The lady Caroline of Baron Rothschild discovered this and expelled Maria Anna who then reluctantly returned to her own parental home, and gave a birth Alois, the father of Hitler. At that time, Caroline and Baron Rothschild had been in discord and separated in the house. It was said that Baron Salomon Rothschild always chased after young women and was lost in lewdness. So, it is very easy to imagine who got Maria Anna, the grandmother of Hitler, pregnant. Consequently, Adolf Hitler's father was an illegitimate child between Baron Salomon Rothschild and Maria Anna, and Hitler was a grandson of Rothschild.

Baron Salomon Rothschild was also said to be the grandfather of Klara, Adolf's mother. That is, Alois and Klara were in a relationship as uncle and niece, and Adolf Hitler was born by the inbreeding. So, he was born as *the product of desire in the Rothschild family* condensing the genetic dominating structure over the two women by undifferentiated sexual desire consciousness based on the instinctive survival consciousnesses. As a result, spiritually, Adolf Hitler was born with his soul containing strong sorrow and ONSHU against the sexual domination by Jews, inherited the mind and soul of a proud Aryan woman, and physically inherited the genes of desires in the Rothschild family.

Because, by the system of the prison star, domination desire and material desire (the instinctive desires) are inherited genetically by male's sperm through the lineage with the positive type superiority, and direct to complete the system of *power, domination, struggle, and destruction.*

Chapter Two ☆ The Deriving Point

The nature of the soul is "decent by conception" by the "rule of the relative original power" based on the sentiment world and spiritual dimension of women, and directs to complete the system of *love, integration, harmony, and creation.* However, inbreeding means that the genetic information regarding the structural arrangement of the genes is strongly repeated, and according to the "rule of the genetic chain" based on the "rule of physical causality," the genetic domination is furthermore increased, so that only the negative information is enriched and minus genetic information will manifest, and it will reverse the evolutional process according to rule of "body is subjective and soul is objective." Since inbreeding increases the genetic domination, and the negative information is duplicated and manifested, the birthrate for mutation, mental disorder and physical disorder, such as mental handicap and physical disability, becomes extremely high. Hitler's half-brothers had a fairly long life, but most of his biological brothers and sisters died in childhood. Law in advanced nations prohibits inbreeding in order to avoid the risks.

The concept of evolution is to reduce genetic domination; the two largest desires based on the instinctive survival consciousnesses, and release the physical desire of the benefits in this world. In order to not deliver abnormal human beings in the future, like Hitler, to this world, and for the further evolution and development of human beings, we should promote global mating beyond the ethnic groups and nations, all over the world, take out the concept of borders and construct a one world family, otherwise, there is no way for human beings to survive. It is proven that many children from international marriages are distinguished and remarkably active in academic and sports fields.

Global crossing will release desires by the instinctive survival consciousnesses remarkably, and suggests the possibility to turn the global collaboration world into a reality in the future to change to the "world one family principle," by abolishing all kinds of discrimination such as racial discrimination, ethnic discrimination and religious discrimination. It will be avoiding conflicts and wars over the benefits of ethnic groups and nations.

Now, I would like to verify the personality formation history of Adolf Hitler and the cause and mechanism of his mental structure. Unless we verify the reason why Adolf Hitler had fallen into nationalism and undergone transformation to persecution and slaughter by being so hostile to the Jewish, we will certainly repeat the same mistake in our history.

There is always motivation in the words and deeds of human beings, and in order to put the motivation in to effect, we must invoke our consciousness, which is done by the "rule of the relative original power" based on the mind and spirit.

The mechanism of invoking the consciousness is this. Everybody contains "soul mind" and "body mind" inside oneself, based on the "rule of the entropy relativity." The qualitative criterion of "soul mind" and "body mind" is different, based on his/her spiritual dimension. The proportion of "soul mind" and "body mind" contained in each person does not differ greatly, because they exist based on the "rule of balance," with the slight fluctuation of imperfection. They are approaching the spiritual evolution, according to the "principle of dimensional integration," by directing to the "soul mind" which is the relative subject. But the big difference is in the

Chapter Two ☆ The Deriving Point

height of spiritual dimension.

The truth of each person exists in the presence of the consciousness, based on SHINSEI, and by invoking the "soul mind" we create a good spirit world, and by invoking the "body mind" we create an evil spirit world, in ourselves. No one else creates a good spirit world or an evil spirit world but your own self. Since the theory of PARAREVO leaves all things to Self-determination, Self-creation and Self-responsibility based on the "rule of freedom," everything is left to the free intention of oneself and Self-responsibility based on Self-creation. So it is totally up to you whether you create a good spirit world or an evil spirit world.

The good consciousness invokes by the "relative original power" between the good spirit world and the "soul mind," and we give words and deeds with good motivation. Of course, the evil consciousness invokes by the relative original power between the evil spirit world and the "body mind" that we have created, and we give words and deeds with evil motivation. Since the cause of invoking the consciousness does not exist outside and everything connotes inside your spiritual consciousness entity of inner-self, *there is no victim consciousness and shifting responsibility existing in the theory of PARAREVO.*

If you do not understand this fundamental rule of the universe, you are not able to verify the nature of human's consciousness. The degree of acceptance of love and freedom of consciousness are different based on the personality formation history, and the criterion of ONSHU and the degree of domination are also different.

At the ethnic level of the "soul mind" dimension filled with love, it will become relative with the good spiritual entity of good ethnic dimension, and people take action of love for the ethnic group, and for a person who has rendered meritorious service at the national level, the good spiritual entity of national dimension will become relative and accomplish a great national achievement.

On the other hand, if the dimension of the "body mind" contained the sorrow and ONSHU, like Adolf Hitler against the Jewish people, the evil spirit entity of the ethnic dimension filled with poor sorrow and ONSHU will become relative, and drive a sense of impulse toward struggle directing to the collapse and destruction of the ethnic group. This relative original power based on the mind and spirit has caused various revolutions, struggles, and wars.

The Aryan nationalism of Adolf Hitler, invoking of consciousness and motivation toward Jewish persecution, are based on the personality formation history and the spiritual formation history of Hitler. Since Hitler had inherited the genes from the Rothschild family, his soul contained domination desire and conquest desire. Sorrow and ONSHU toward the Jewish had been inherited spiritually in his soul by the mental world and the spiritual dimension of Aryan women. By combining the sorrow and ONSHU of his soul and the domination desire and struggle desire in the body, the human character called Adolf Hitler was born and appeared in this world. And, since women have the power of creation as their nature, the harmful energy of his foolish mistress, Eva Braun, pushed him to create further violence and tragedy between Germans and Jews by the opposite ONSHU. Indeed, it is not an exaggeration to say that Adolf Hitler was *the child of sorrow and ONSHU of Mary Magdalene* who was deprived of her beloved Jesus by the Jews.

Since the genetic code in the lineage is completed in the three

Chapter Two ☆ The Deriving Point

generations in this world, by the "rule of preservation by inscription," it is possible to verify the spiritual wave in the spiritual dimension, which is relative to the person, by analyzing the instinctive remaining consciousness in the three generations of parents, children, and grandchildren. Especially between parents and grandchildren, the physical domination in the causality manifest strongly.

The three generations from Adolf Hitler was his grandfather Baron Salomon Rothschild, and he had the greatest influence on Adolf Hitler, spiritually and physically. Therefore, by analyzing and verifying the mental world and the spiritual dimension of Baron Salomon Rothschild, it might be possible to understand Hitler's invoked consciousness and motivation route on the mind and spirit, both inside and outside.

I can analyze psychologically, Baron Salomon Rothschild from two points of view, the mental world and the spiritual dimension. Even though he was a millionaire Baron with no inconvenience, he held fear and anxiety, not to Aryan, Anglo-Saxon, French, or Italian, but to Jewish financial combines and the Jews themselves who had spread through Europe and would surely gain power and emerge throughout the world. It was *the power of the family consciousness by the relative original power* that invoked this consciousness of fear and anxiety. In fact, the Rothschild family had connected and succeeded the lineage by inbreeding. It was worse than royal families. It is easy to understand their exclusiveness by seeing the facts. They were so afraid of the invasion of their privacy that they excluded and strongly refused other lineages.

In a foreign land called America, Italian mafia and Chinese mafia have rarely killed and had conflicts with other ethnic groups for their supremacy. It is understandable if they compete with the mafia of other ethnic groups for supremacy, but for some reason, they have only repeated the conflicts and killings for supremacy among the same ethnic groups. It is easy to derive the relative original power among the same ethnic groups, but it is hard to invoke the consciousness to derive the relative original power based on the mind and the spirit, and the motivation to action with other ethnics groups, because there has been no existence of spiritual relativity, historically between ethnic groups.

When we are in Japan, we are not aware of Japanese at all, but once we are abroad, we are aware of Japanese in the unconscious mind. We have a stronger connection with the existence that is closer by the relative wave and derive greater relative original power. It is like we feel closer plants than minerals, animals than plants, and human beings than animals.

As we can see from this fact, the most fear, insecurity, and terror Baron Salomon Rothschild felt were not against other ethnic groups or foreigners. He had fears that someday he would be forced out from the position of millionaire by Jews and Jewish financial combines because of conflicts for rights and supremacy among Jews in Europe in the future. It is an unquestionable fact that the economy in the world is still made a fool of between the two Jewish financial combines of Rothschild family and Rockefeller family, by being dragged into conflicts for rights and supremacy. For Salomon Rothschild, the Jews were the only uncomfortable and inconvenient existence, and he died being caught in his own trap of power and wealth, holding fear and anxiety toward Jews, and became a bounded ghost. Thus, the personality (mind) of Adolf Hitler and the

Chapter Two ☆ The Deriving Point

spirituality (soul) of Salomon Rothschild were relatively connected, and by the "rule of the relative original power" based on the mind and spirit, the consciousness of fear and insecurity were amplified and invoked, then, according to the motivation to ostracize all Jews in Europe, Hitler had them executed.

If Adolf Hitler did not have the Rothschild family behind him, he could not become the dictator Adolf Hitler in one generation. He would not be that kind of person only by his intention and Self-effort. As a matter of fact, such bizarre behavior of dictators who invoked the consciousness from insecurity and fear can be seen in many places in the world.

Mao Zedong, for instance, purged more than 20 million of his fellow intellectuals, artists, and highly educated people under the Great Cultural Revolution in China. There was also genocide in the Baltic's, by Stalin in the former Soviet Union, and forced labor in Siberia, etc. More recently, there was genocide by chemical weapons and poison gas against the Kurdish under the dictatorship of Saddam Hussein in Iraq.

Like those, ugly behaviors such as revolutions and riots became phenomenon by the relative original power between the fear of coward dictators and mass hysteria of public from complaints and dissatisfaction.

Another reason is that Baron Salomon Rothschild had a problem in his personality formation history. Because of his wealth, he could not grow with maternal love and a decent home environment. In the Jewish values, they always want to show off a symbol of power and wealth when they become rich, so I could say that they were easy to fall into sexual disgrace by undifferentiated sexual desire consciousness in the male type sexual dominating structure. They have become depraved by sexual dominating activity between love desire toward maternity and sexual desire toward women. Baron Salomon Rothschild 's father did the same things and built the pile of sorrow and ONSHU of many women in the lineage history.

This sorrow and ONSHU were aggregated by inbreeding, and the sperm of Alois was bound with the ovum of Klara, and the womb of Klara was opened to receive the soul of Adolf Hitler. Then the soul of Hitler, which contained sorrow and ONSHU of women toward Jews, descended to the womb of Klara from the spiritual world, by conception.

The historical sorrow and ONSHU of women against the male type sexual dominating structure of Jews were aggregated and spiritually inherited from Maria Anna to Klara, and then Adolf Hitler was born as *a child of sorrow and ONSHU* based on the *thought of hatred* of women. He was born carrying the background of spiritual ONSHU of Jews, and grew up in a contradictory duality of blind love and ONSHU by being doted on by his Aryan mother.

Adolf Hitler was born containing multiple personality factors. Inside of him, there were two physical and spiritual ethnic groups, which were totally different and opposite. This was the main cause and problem for Jews, and it had existed in the Jews themselves as an essential core of ONSHU. Hitler just changed and substituted it to the nationalism of the Nazis. Hitler himself was only a piece of work. The author who delivered and raised him with his spiritual background and lineage, are more important than the piece of work itself, so we should also verify the lineage of the author who produced him.

Chapter Two ☆ The Deriving Point

Adolf Hitler marvelously completed the nature of Baron Salomon Rothschild, his grandfather, as the lineage of three generations. Salomon Rothschild was a Jewish millionaire in Vienna, and indeed, he was just like King Solomon who had built the Solomon Empire in the Old Testament. Salomon and Solomon have the same derivation, but are pronounced differently depending on the language.

Theoretical frameworks and values of Jewish are based on the Old Testament, and King Solomon was the symbol of power and wealth. Solomon preferred luxury and a gluttonous life, and had 700 wives and 300 concubines. It is easy to understand that the symbol of his power and wealth was the domination of many women. It is exactly the same as the sexual domination world of apes, chimpanzee bonobos, which are considered to be the most human-like. Also the Jews believe it is the great blessing of God, so I could say that the Jewish God is exactly *the God of physical world benefits*.

Even now, two thirds of the global wealth is in complete control of the Jewish millionaires, and the world economy is in their hands. The original idea based on the theoretical frameworks and values of Jewish is that poor people are not blessed by God, and rich people are the ones who do receive blessing from God, so it seems to me that they completely distinguish, and discriminate against the people. The Old Testament is *the book of the God of the physical world benefits* that had been written of debauchery, slaughter, and taking love, according to polygamy, that legalized the male type sexual desire domination structure. Also, harmful influence of polygamy based on undifferentiated sexual desire consciousness is to take the freedom of women away, infringe on love, and inherit the emotion of ONSHU spiritually.

Sorrow and ONSHU in the triangle relationship between Abraham, Sarah, and Hagar was the source that derived the ONSHU of Ishmael and Isaac and continuously built the history of struggle and slaughter between Israel people, who represent Judaism, and the Arabs, who represent Islam, which continuing to this day. And the triangle relationship of sorrow and ONSHU between Salomon Rothschild, Caroline, and Mary Anna manifested the genealogy of love and hatred and ONSHU as a correlation between Nazis and Jewish.

As Sarah banished Hagar to the wilderness, Caroline expelled Mary Anna when she was pregnant. At that time, proud Aryan Mary Anna cursed the Rothschild family and the Jewish, which were the symbol of power and wealth in arrogant Jewish male type sexual desire domination structure, and raised Alois in her womb and delivered him to this world. Alois deeply absorbed the ONSHU of Mary Anna as spiritual nourishment and created the core of his personal framework with ONSHU in her womb. Like his father, Alois had marital relationships with three women by the male type sexual desire domination structure.

The result of ONSHU of Mary Anna was the marriage of Alois with Klara. Klara is also an Aryan woman who had contained ONSHU toward the arrogant Rothschild family and Jews by inheriting the lineage of Rothschild. Alois, who had fully absorbed maternal love and hate of Mary Anna, and Klara who had inherited ONSHU of the mistress as the third generation from Rothschild, had more than enough interrelation of ONSHU to meet each

Chapter Two ☆ The Deriving Point

other in fate. Also, it was the time and background to change the ONSHU relationship between Mary Anna and Caroline to ethnic discrimination, and to form the hostility structure.

It is because Germany was defeated in World War I and had been alienated and isolated in Europe during the depression. In this backdrop, Jews were highlighted, boasting remarkable economy, and had outrageous behavior. The stress and frustration caused by jealousy and envy had accumulated in the country, so that it was the best timely background to provide an outlet of the complaints and dissatisfaction toward Jews.

But Nazi's ethnic discrimination against Jews was only superficial. The core of ONSHU, which was the essential cause, was in the ethnic customs of Jews and legalized discrimination against women in the male type sexual desire domination structure represented by Baron Rothschild. It was also the challenge and revolution against Jews by proud Aryan women who were fed up with such a Self-righteous and arrogant male type sexual desire domination structure.

The true discrimination in human history is neither racism nor nation discrimination nor religions discrimination. The core of the true discrimination is sexism against women. It has continued to exist at the bottom of various discriminations, so that the discrimination inside discriminations is the one against women.

The seed of ONSHU against the Jews is deeply imbedded in Christianity. Since they put Jesus Christ, the Messiah, on the cross and executed him, Jews are thought of as the sinful race.

As a consequence, the real *struggle of Hitler* was not the matters written in "Mein Kampf" but the cultural struggle of the two ethnics, which were connoted inside him. It contained spiritual

ONSHU of women in the soul, and it was about abolition of sexism against women in the Jewish, male type sexual desire domination structure that was the core of internal ONSHU, and a challenge to the God of physical world benefits.

Most saints, righteous people, and tyrants such as David, Solomon, Jesus, Buddha, and Gandhi were delivered to this world by sorrow and ONSHU in the triangle relationship.

★See diagrams "The system of sorrow and ONSHU in the triangle relationship" on P179, P180

The system of sorrow and ONSHU in the triangle relationship
Lineage of Jacob (1)

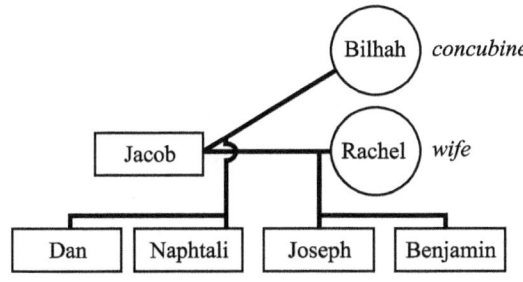

Lineage of Jacob (2)

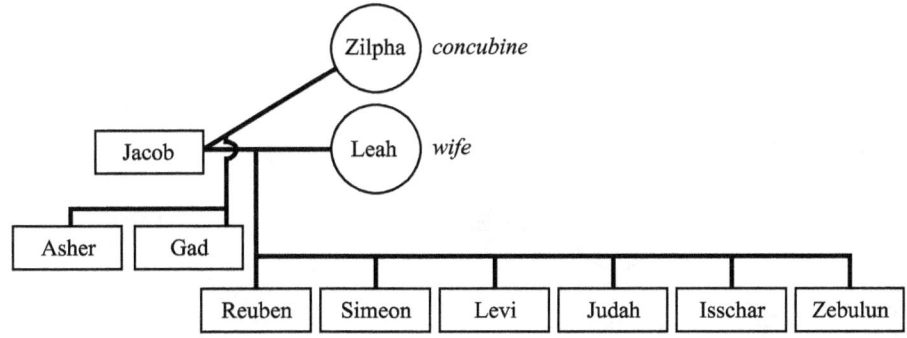

Chapter Two ☆ The Deriving Point

The system of sorrow and ONSHU in the triangle relationship

Lineage of Adam

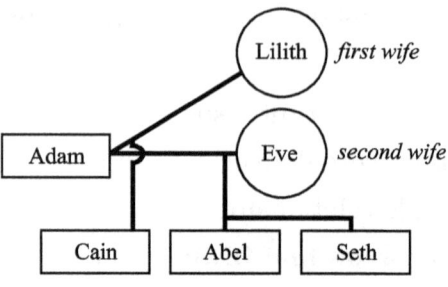

Linage of Rothschild

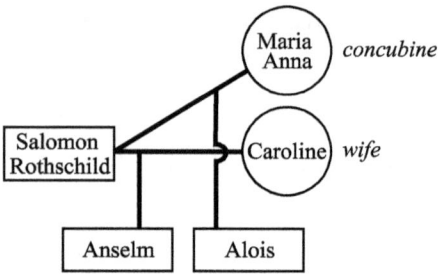

Lineage of Abraham

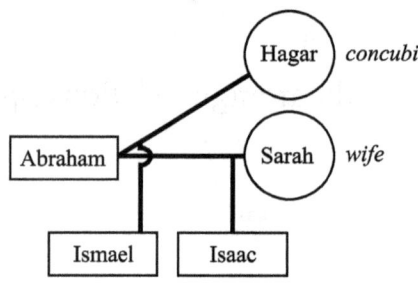

Linage of Adolf Hitler

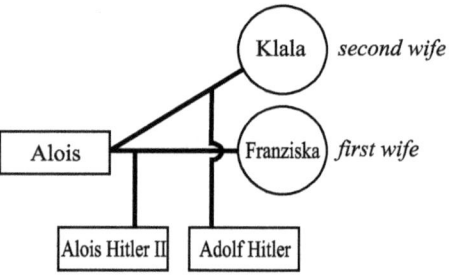

Lineage of Jesus Christ

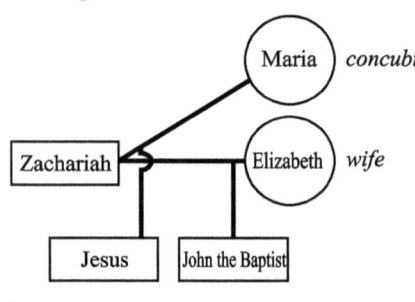

Linage of Izanagi (The KOJIKI)

Lineage of David

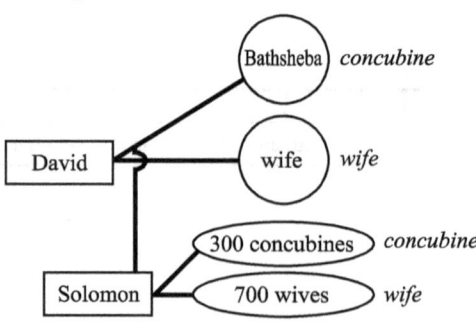

Linage of Buddha

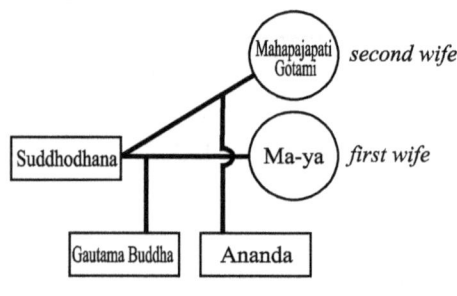

2-72. The "rule of sorrow and ONSHU in the triangle relationship" in Jacob's family

The "rule of sorrow and ONSHU in the triangle relationship" in the family of Jacob is as follows. Jacob and Esau, the twins who were born between Isaac, the son of Abraham, and Rebekah, had been fighting fiercely inside Rebekah's womb until the moment they were born. After they were born in this world, the younger brother Jacob took the privilege of eldest son from Esau, and by the wisdom of his mother. Jacob deprived Esau of his father's blessing, and having to escape Esau's anger, stayed with Rebekah's elder brother, Uncle Laban.

There, Jacob did his best and increased Uncle Laban's wealth and possessions using his wisdom, even though Laban deceived Jacob ten times. Laban had two daughters, Leah, the elder daughter, and Rachel, the second daughter. Jacob loved the beautiful daughter Rachel. For her love, he had to serve Laban for seven years. But he was deceived by Laban again and had to marry Leah.

He and Leah had four children, Reuben, Simeon, Levi and Judah. Jacob served Laban for seven more years, and then finally, he could marry Rachel. However, Rachel was barren, so she gave him her maid Biruha who conceived two children named Dan and Naphtali. That prompted Rachel to conceive her legitimate children Joseph and Benjamin.

After bearing four children, Leah could no longer conceive, so Leah gave Jacob her maid Zilpah who conceived two children named Gad and Asher. After that, although she was infertile once, Leah became pregnant and delivered two more children named Zebulun and Issachar. Because of sorrow and ONSHU in the triangle relationship between Jacob, Leah and Zilpah, Leah conceived six legitimate children, and Zilpah conceived two illegitimate children, all fathered by Jacob. And, because of sorrow and ONSHU in the triangle relationship between Jacob, Rachel and Biruha, Rachel conceived two legitimate children, and Biruha conceived two illegitimate children. Of course, there was sorrow and ONSHU in the triangle relationship between the wives, Leah and Rachel with Jacob as well.

In the end, Jacob had twelve children by the four women. From these twelve children, the twelve tribes of Israel were formed.

After that, Jacob surpassed Esau`s ONSHU by love and transcended his "body mind," and Jacob was renamed, Israel, the title of the triumph of love. Later, the brothers were emotionally integrated and united.

2-73. Trial and persecution produce spiritual evolution and prosperity

Of course, Israel loved Rachel `s children more than those from Leah, Zilpah, and Biruha. He loved Joseph the most, more than any of the other children, because he got him when he was older. By ONSHU and jealousy according to the "rule of jealousy exclusive theory," Joseph`s half-brothers talked about to killing him. However, with the suggestion from Judah, they decided to sell him to the Ishmael people, as a slave, for 20 silver shekels. The Ishmael people took him to Egypt and sold him to a captain of the guard Potiphar, who was an official of the Pharaoh, the king of Egypt. Joseph did not give in to sexual temptation from the mistress, the wife of the captain of the guard, and although he was imprisoned by her perjury, he brought his ability as a prophet into play in prison, and soon became known by the Pharaoh. Later he interpreted a dream of the Pharaoh predicting that seven years harvest and seven years famine would come to Egypt. As the prophet Joseph, he saved Egypt from the famine and was promoted to prime minister of Egypt.

So, Joseph accepted the worst situation and environment with love by the "rule of entropy relativity" and rose to the highest level.

2-74. Love and ONSHU are inherited by sentiments of women

As we can see in the Old Testament, love and ONSHU of the triangle relationship between Jacob, Leah and Zilpah, and between Jacob, Rachel and Biruha had expanded into ONSHU and jealousy in their children. Naturally, the core of sorrow and ONSHU of the women toward Jacob was the struggle for supremacy as a wife, between Rachel and Leah, in the triangle relationship between the three of them.

The "rule of sorrow and ONSHU in the triangle relationship" based on the "earth logical evidence," had consistently been inherited with the women's sentiment world and the genetic code, physically and spiritually, throughout history. It also succeeded to descendants by the "rule of reincarnation and genetic chain" based on the "rule of causality."

When an infertile woman transcends her ONSHU by love, she is able to open her womb by releasing her ONSHU, then can

Chapter Two ☆ The Deriving Point

receive her loving husband's seeds (sperm) according to the "rule of relative original power" with the mind and spirit. So she can restore the right of inheritance to her legitimate children. From incidents in the Old Testament, by transcending her own ONSHU and surpassing with love, then by giving her own maidservant the right of inheritance, causing her to conceive illegitimate children, I believe there is a mechanism for infertile women to conceive a legitimate child from the spiritual world. The system to continue the lineage, by this mechanism is in the PARAREVO theory.

We have heard many times that when childless couples adopted children, they conceived their own biological child. For instance, in Japan's history, in the Royal family and the Shogun family, it was a custom for the successor to have concubines conceive his children, and then the legal wife conceived a legitimate son.

Since the "equation of the universe" is *by loving ONSHU, releasing one's own ONSHU, then opening one's own fate based on the "rule of entropy relativity,"* it becomes possible to prepare and make ready the fundamental feeling to receive a soul, the spiritual consciousness entity, by giving one's beloved husband to another woman by surpassing one's own ONSHU by love and by opening one's own womb of ONSHU.

Based on the "rule of entropy relativity," it is possible for totally opposed spiritual consciousness entities to impregnate the soul that is relative to one's own feelings, from the spiritual world, based on the "rule of relative original power" with the mind and spirit. Thus, the conflict relationship of incompatible legitimate and illegitimate children, between the wife and the concubine, will be inevitably contained in each illegitimate and legitimate child's soul, and born to this world with it, then with Self-determination, they will shoulder the role and responsibility to release the ONSHU and discord, in this world.

Also based on the "rule of balance," as we can see by the incidents of Jacob and Joseph, there is unseen influence and blessing from a higher spiritual dimension, and it will derive and inevitably become relative to the mental world and the personality dimension, which transcended tribulation and persecution by love by the "rule of the relative original power" with the mind and spirit, so fate will be directed to the higher stage.

Even Adam, Abraham, and Jacob had only completed the role and responsibility to plant the physical seed by leaving it to undifferentiated sexual desire consciousness. However, the right of inheritance of the soul that was the lineage of spiritual consciousness entity in history is determined and completed by the spiritual sentiment world and personality dimension of women. And the right of inheritance of the body is determined by the negative type superiority and by the genetic code of ovum; so that the right to determine and the right of inheritance are left in the sentiment world and personality dimension of women, whether the lineage continuously exists over descendants, or becomes extinct.

Therefore, human beings have historically achieved spiritual and physical evolution by completing lineage conversion by women. In the history of the royal family and the Shogun family, there is nothing other than having been trapped in the male heir system, and having built up a pile of ONSHU, discord, and sorrow toward women, over the heirs of sons through the wives and concubines. Since men do not have the lineage right to inheritance spiritually or physically, we have done totally meaningless and purposeless male line inheritance, and only built a pile of ONSHU toward women in the lineages. If we want to maintain excellent lineage, we should transfer to female line inheritance and pass the right of inheritance to women who are spiritually superior and wise, and should maintain the evolutionary lineage.

Even now, ignorant male line advocates in the male type domination structure try to continue the unfortunate chain by the negative spiral of married women.

2-75. Love pillage by King David and ONSHU of Uriah

King David had many wives and concubines. One day at dusk, when David was walking on the roof of his palace, he saw below, a woman bathing. She was elegant and very beautiful, but she was Bathsheba, the wife of Uriah. Uriah was a serious and honest soldier and very loyal to King David. But David had fallen in love with her, and in order to have her for his own, he sent Uriah to the most severe battlefield and legally had him killed. Since Uriah was killed in action, Bathsheba accepted David's favor. However, David's conduct was dominated by undifferentiated sexual desire consciousness, which incurred God's anger, and their first son only survived for a few months after his birth.

The second child, who was born by the pillaging love of David, was Solomon. He reached the summit of his splendor as King Solomon, but became a prisoner of material and sexual desires so he had a life of lust and corruption, loving the magnificent life, covered with gold and silver treasures, and had 700 wives and 300 concubines.

Later, the Kingdom of Solomon was divided into the Northern dynasty Israel and the Southern dynasty Judah. It is like drawing the exact picture of development of the male type sexual desire domination structure. I can hardly believe the Old Testament is the holy book of God's providence. All I can see is a figure of a greedy God, which devoted himself only to the physical world benefits.

2-76. Analysis of the personality formation history of Jesus Christ

There was a priest who had an important position in Judaism, named Zacharias. His wife's name was Elizabeth, and the couple was righteous before God. However, the couple could not conceive children, just like Abraham and Sarah, and Jacob and Rachel. Also, Zacharias and Elizabeth were old like the other two couples. Elizabeth was a sterile woman with a firmly closed womb, just like Sarah and Rachel. An angel appeared to Zacharias just like the angel did to Abraham and he was given predictions exactly the same way. However, Elizabeth was old and she did not have menstruation anymore, so it was impossible for her to conceive a child.

At that time, in Zacharias's home, Elizabeth's relative Mary, who later became the mother of Jesus, served as a maid. In those days, the male type sexual domination and undifferentiated sexual desire consciousness dominated, so Zacharias and Mary began a relationship of undifferentiated sexual impulse and as a result of the sexual relationship, *Mary conceived Jesus.* In the Jewish religious laws at that time, with discrimination against women, women who committed adultery were supposed to be executed by

Chapter Two ☆ The Deriving Point

stoning. But, since Mary was her relative, Elizabeth removed Mary from their home as if nothing happened, and released her. This is the big difference between Sarah and Elizabeth.

Later, Mary married Joseph while she was pregnant and gave birth to Jesus. Then, Elizabeth became pregnant, opening her closed womb, even though she was too old to get pregnant. Then, she gave birth to John the Baptist. So, *Jesus and John the Baptist were half-brothers* and later they had a fateful meeting. In Zacharias's family, Jesus, the illegitimate child, and John the Baptist, the legitimate child, were born by the "rule of sorrow and ONSHU in the triangle relationship" between Zacharias, Elizabeth, and Mary.

Fundamentally, the personality formation should be made by Self-completion, and conception by descent, "love pair-system of SHINSEI unity" based on the "cosmological evidence," however, the "earth logical evidence" has left the role and responsibility to women's spiritual evolution in the sentiment world and spiritual dimension based on the "rule of sorrow and ONSHU in the triangle system."

We have a choice of whether we build a chain of unhappiness by sorrow and ONSHU of women as we have done continuously throughout history, or we open the path to the spiritual evolution by releasing ONSHU by loving the ONSHU itself. However, human beings left it as a fingerprint of history by the sexual relationships based on the sexual desire consciousness, so it has been inherited in the souls of the next generation by sorrow and ONSHU of women, and has inherited the physical desires by the sperm of men, so we repeated struggles and slaughters.

Alois, the father of Adolf Hitler, was the child of Mary Anna who worked as a maid for the Rothschild family. (See 2-71 for more details about Hitler). Just like Sarah, who banished Hagar and Ishmael to the wilderness, Salomon's wife Caroline banished Mary Anna from the Rothschild family even though she was pregnant. This was similar to the incident when Elizabeth relieved Mary from Zacharias's home while she was pregnant with Jesus. As a result, Mary Anna gave birth to Alois, holding strong sorrow and ONSHU.

The qualitative dimension, the nature of a conceived soul, is determined by the "rule of the relative original power" with the mind and spirit based on the sentiment world and the spiritual dimension in a mother's sexual conception relationship. The real personality formation would not be completed without prenatal environment based on free love and an ideal environment of love in the earth life. The opposite process of the spiritual evolution and the history of struggle and destruction have been built by the sentiment world and the spiritual dimension of women. The roles and responsibilities of the men in the prison star are to legalize the "principle of dimensional domination" and build an inconvenient society. *The "sorrow and ONSHU in the triangle system" has built the pyramidal social structure in history, which is considered the typical pattern of exploiting side and exploited side in the male type sexual domination structure.*

From the family to society and nations in the world, all functions are systematized by the mechanism of the pyramidal domination structure.

However, in *the "love pair-system of SHINSEI unity"* based on the "cosmological evidence," it is not a vertical three points rule but a horizontal two points rule, so it can build a smooth spherical

Chapter Two ☆ The Deriving Point

type social structure with the focus of SHINSEI. The whole entire universe is completed and integrated by the "love pair-system," depending on each spiritual dimension, by the relative universal original power based on free love. The universe directs to the sustainable existence forming harmony and order with the spherical motion, while building the spherical structure.

If Jesus was not an illegitimate child who was born by the "sorrow and ONSHU in the earth logical triangle system," but was born and grew up in an ideal family with the "love pair-system" based on the PARAREVO theory, he could have had the view of life and death based on the rule of "spirit is subjective and body is objective," and would never have said "Father, please forgive them" referring to Jewish and the Roman soldiers, concluding they were the culprits, by the "principle of dimensional domination" by external separation. If Jesus was born to this world by the "love pair-system" and had completed "the love pair-system of SHINSEI unity" with an ideal woman, and as a couple had built a family, the earth star would be an ideal world, and we could have constructed a smooth spherical social structure by Christianity all over the world, and the global collaboration would have been completed already.

However, as an example, the United States, the largest Christian nation, is still at the forefront of wars, which proves the fact that our world is not yet completed. History proves as undeniable fact, that Jewish society, Christian society, and Muslim society have built the pyramidal dominating structure by the hierarchy system such as the Pope, priests, and rabbis, by the male type dominating structure.

In this way, in the whole society, everything is commanded

and operated by the pyramidal dominating structure, such as the bureaucratic governing structure, the military, the Self-Defense Forces and the police, as a symbol of state power, and religious groups which are supposed to be the spiritual support, and corporate organizations. The nature of the earth star is that *sexual desire domination changes to conquest desire domination.*

The undeniable fact exists that Jesus and John the Baptist were also forced to be born as illegitimate and legitimate children by the "sorrow and ONSHU in the triangle system," between Zacharias, Elizabeth and Mary, based on the "earth logical evidence," and has continuously built the pyramidal organization in Christian churches.

★**See diagrams "Earth logical Triangle System"**
  "Cosmological Pair System" on P192

2-77. Historical lessons in the Bible

As we can see from the incidents in the Bible, the "rule of sorrow and ONSHU in the triangle relationship" clearly manifested the male type dominating structure based on the instinctive survival consciousnesses, according to the "earth logical evidence." The Old Testament explains the interrelation between the sexual desire and the domination desire, and the interrelation between the dietary desire and the material desire, which are contained as a fate of the prison planet, the earth, and left by logos (language) as the book of *the God of physical world benefits* as a fingerprint of history.

It also clearly suggests by the female type integrating structure, how we have gone through the spiritual evolution by surpassing

Chapter Two ☆ The Deriving Point

Earth Logical Triangle System | Cosmological Pair System

oxygen domination structure of water molecule | **integration structure of superparticle**

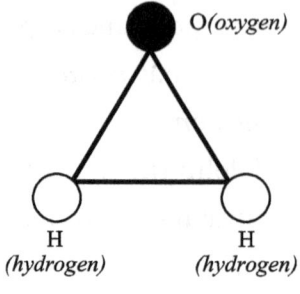 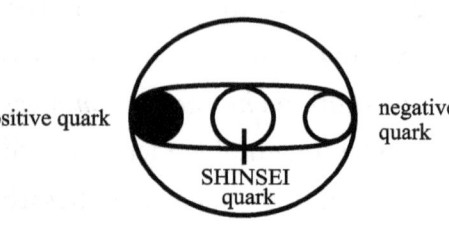

body domination structure | **SHINSEI integration structure**

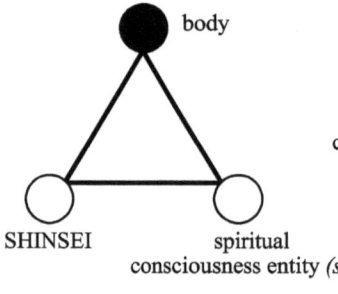 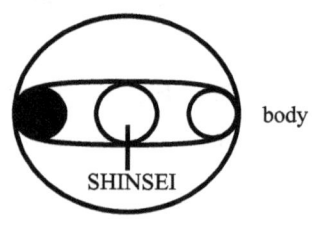

male type domination structure | **man and woman unity type integration**

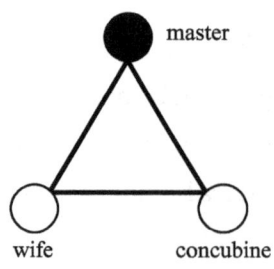 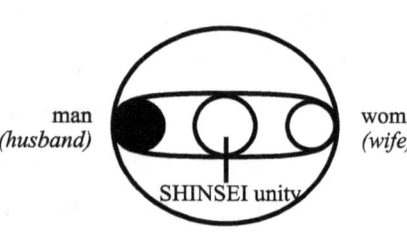

pyramid type domination structure | **sphere type integration structure**

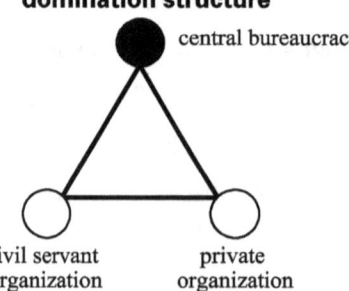 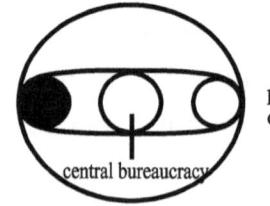

and integrating sorrow and ONSHU by spiritually wise women, with love, who have been used and abused by men. The role and responsibility of men and women on the earth star, are directed and clarified by the opposite theory, based on the "rule of the entropy relativity." The men's theory of the role and responsibility on the prison planet is *power, domination, struggle and destruction,* and, contrarily, the women's theory is *love, integration, harmony and creation.*

Women are directed to dependence and domination, legally, by the male type sexual desire dominating structure and material desire dominating structure, so everything is systematized to direct to inconvenience by the mechanism to complete *the "principle of dependence and domination."* Women have been striving for release from the male type sexual and material dominating structure, and the prison star, by integrating and surpassing ONSHU with love in the history of trials and tribulations. In those processes, many women have sacrificed, but still brought the spiritual evolution by directing the generation and development of human beings throughout history.

The male type dominating structure has played the role and responsibility as the mechanism and system of domination, and the female type integrating structure by sentiment world and spiritual dimension of spiritually wise women's maternal love that has played the role and responsibility as the system of the spiritual evolution.

According to the "rule of sorrow and ONSHU in the triangle relationship," the contents of Adam and Eve in the lost paradise were rewritten for men's convenience in order to legalize the male type dominating structure. By reversing the sexual desire and

Chapter Two ☆ The Deriving Point

the dietary desire, which have been contained as the instinctive survival consciousnesses from the primitive life entity as fate, men have developed impossible theories such as Eve was deceived by a snake. It has painted women as unfaithful and filthy sinners and directed the male type dominating structure to superiority in order to accomplish the role and responsibility of the prison star. So, to accomplish that, the male dominating society made women out to be the ringleaders of sin, and men have committed to legally murder women because of unfaithful and sinful behavior, denied the existence of women in society and history, and tried to close the path to spiritual evolution.

Hiding the genitals by covering them with a fig leaf is an epoch-making behavior of the spiritual evolution in the sexual differentiation. However, it was interpreted by the theory of original sin by Augustine as totally opposite and has been treated as sinful behavior of Adam and Eve. Since Adam was dominated by undifferentiated sexual impulse by the male sexual desire consciousness, and had a tumultuous sexual relationship with Lilith, Cain was born to this world by the "rule of sorrow and ONSHU in the triangle relationship." Under the male sexual desire domination and material domination, it has been the history of sorrow and ONSHU of women who have desperately tried to receive souls from a higher spiritual dimension. This triangle system has complicated the problems of love, and put the morality, ethics and separation of sex in a low-dimension. And this undifferentiated sexual desire became the root of evil and has prevented us from making spiritual evolution.

In order to play the role of the prison star, we have legalized the triangle system in which men are at the top of the system, and expanded the vertical structure of the male type domination from family to society, ethnics, nation and world, and constructed the pyramidal social structure in the world.

What the tree of life and tree of the knowledge of good and evil in the Garden of Eden had expressed metaphorically, is as follows: The tree of life represents women who had directed to freedom, release, and evolution by the "principle of dimensional integration" by internal separation, and conceived and sent the spiritual consciousness entities, as children, to this world, based on the rule of "spirit is subjective and body is objective," and contained the theory of *love, integration, harmony, and creation.* The tree of the knowledge of good and evil represents men who had directed to inconvenience, domination, and oppression, that was the instinctive survival consciousness by the "principle of dimensional domination" by external separation, and strengthened the evil competition principle by "the theory of good and evil" and "the theory of merit" based on the rule of "body is subjective and spirit is objective," and contained the theory of *power, domination, struggle, and destruction.*

So, the female type integrating structure, the tree of life, builds the integration type society based on love of "soul mind," and surely symbolizes women who reproduce life by *the "rule of change by birth and re-birth,"* and direct to eternal life by guiding to the spiritual evolution. And the male type dominating structure, the tree of the knowledge of good and evil, is the source of the worldly benefits based on the desire of "body mind" and builds the struggle type society with "the theory of good and evil" and "the theory of merit," and surely symbolizes the men who direct to inconvenience by

Chapter Two ☆ The Deriving Point

legalizing the dominating structure of the prison star.

If men surrender obediently to women and accept women's opinion sincerely, humbly, and modestly, in order to release historical sorrow and ONSHU of women, and integrate to love of women, the path to the spiritual evolution will be opened to us, and it will be possible to reach the cosmic life entity, which is the eternal spiritual life entity.

In order for men to accomplish Self-completion to bring the personality formation to a higher dimension, they do not need to practice a monastic or Buddhist life like traditional religions, and they do not need to pilgrimage in search of hardship and difficulty, living a single life.

The real equation for personality formation based on the "cosmological evidence" is to repent the male type dominating structure, truly and sincerely, and to release sorrow and ONSHU by serving women faithfully and to construct *"ideal love pair-system of SHINSEI unity"* by being integrated with the love of spiritually wise women. The "cosmological evidence" is trying to complete *the "SHINSEI integration life entity"* directing to a smooth spherical type integrating structure by the "love pair-system of SHINSEI unity," based on the love of SHINSEI.

If we sincerely hold the common existing purpose and existing value and want to graduate from the earth star in this life time and want to become a life entity in the huge infinite universe, when we get tired of living just to live, being busy from beginning to end by being dominated by the "instinctive survival consciousnesses," we should create the "Heaven" that is the nation for two people, and integrate the key and keyway for opening the door to the "Heaven" by love. Otherwise, we won't be able to graduate from the earth star forever.

Up to the 20th century, there have been too many ignorant women who have surrendered to the male type dominating structure. Also, if thoughtless women like Cleopatra, Marie Antoinette and Empress Dowager Cixi stand on the dominating side by using men, it only builds a tragic history. Therefore, we are eagerly awaiting the birth of spiritually wise women of SHINSEI unity, as a cry of Gaia.

I previously mentioned that the worst discrimination on the earth star is sexism against women. But the world will never change as long as women continue to have victim consciousness. It is the common purpose and assignment for all women in this life to release ONSHU against men by changing their victim consciousness to "wrongdoer consciousness," which means to regret and admonish oneself like a wrongdoer, according to "the rule of relative conversion." Based on Self-determination, women chose the sexuality as women in this life.

Contents for Book 3 : Chapter Three ☆ The Turning point

3-1. Limit of the finite theory of the universe
3-2. Universe is the perfect collaboration
3-3. "Relative universal original power" and proof of relativity of the universe
3-4. SHINSEI (true sense) and the "rule of original creation power" in the universe
3-5. SHINSEI is not the only and absolute existence
3-6. The views of God dispelled by the PARAREVO theory
3-7. Mechanisms of infinity of the universe
3-8. Imperfection of the relative fluctuation is the driving force for evolution
3-9. The "rule of preservation by inscription" based on "All worldly things are impermanent"
3-10. Physical world benefits and spiritual world benefits are the opposite sides of the coin
3-11. Energy waves in material world and spiritual world
3-12. Memory is always trying to preserve higher inscription
3-13. The complex three-dimensional structure of SHINSEI, the soul, and the body
3-14. The definition and the rules of SHINSEI
3-15. Spiritual world benefits and physical world benefits based on the principle of freedom
3-16. The "rule of reincarnation" is the curse and bind of instinctive survival consciousnesses
3-17. The "rule of relative conversion" in the qualitative world and the quantitative world
3-18. The "rule of reincarnation" of the quantitative world in the earth star
3-19. The qualitative world and quantitative world are reverse vector
3-20. The importance of verifying the spiritual dimension
3-21. The universe directs to dimensional integration
3-22. The PARAREVO theory and the equations for spiritual evolution
3-23. The criterion of love in the sentiment world determines the 10 levels of spiritual dimensions
3-24. Gradual stages of the sentiment world in the spiritual dimension

3-25. The criterion of mind and spirit determines the 10 levels of spiritual consciousness entities
3-26. The 10 levels of the criterion of physical desire
3-27. The criterion of spirit and mind of the 6 stages in the level of the earth
3-28. The equation for "regeneration of SHINSEI and soul"
3-29. The relative original power with trinity of Sun, Moon, and Earth
3-30. Substantial relative original power with the Moon
3-31. The energy wave of the Moon and atomic conversion
3-32. The difference of physical effects between the new moon and the full moon
3-33. Possible methods to make energy conversion of water molecules
3-34. Dependency on water and the principle of domination
3-35. The world of SHINSEI integration consciousness is infinite
3-36. The release of the body from oxygen domination
3-37. Hydrogen was the first element in the universe
3-38. Excessive oxygen domination makes active oxygen
3-39. Ancient lives succeeded in obtaining oxygen
3-40. Mechanism of respiration and oxidation
3-41. The energy wave of the moon is the border between the spiritual world and this world
3-42. Roles and responsibilities of the moon toward the earth
3-43. Solar energy waves affect the mind
3-44. Solar energy waves are feminine "negative" nature
3-45. True Self-discovery is to discover SHINSEI
3-46. Excessive desire consciousness and the brain dominating structure
3-47. Five conditions for spiritual evolution
3-48. The blind spot of the Mobius loop of "vertical love" and the core of ONSHU
3-49. Love and ONSHU between parents and children have distorted the sexual differentiation
3-50. The blind spot of the Mobius loop of "horizontal love" and the core of ONSHU of brothers and sisters
3-51. The blind spot in the Mobius loop of "horizontal love" and the core of ONSHU of husband and wife
3-52. The 21st century is the creative era of spiritually wise women
3-53. Horizontal love of the Mobius loop and integration of sexuality

3-54. Pair system of love in the SHINSEI unity
3-55. History has been built with the love and ONSHU of women
3-56. Chakras are "spiritual organs" to integrate the soul and the body
3-57. Release of chakras and spiritual dimensions
3-58. Dysfunction of chakras occurs by unpleasant feelings
3-59. The time required for disembodiment and spiritual dimensions
3-60. Chakra adjustment methods of resuscitation by Self-reliance and reliance upon others
3-61. The level of releasing chakras determines the direction of spiritual dimensions
3-62. Verification of sexual integration and sexual anomaly
3-63. The methods to surpass and transcend sexual anomalies
3-64. Chakras will disappear in the intangible world
3-65. The relative wave based on the spiritual dimension and the principle of the relative original power
3-66. Power of the collective consciousness by the relative original power
3-67. The relative original power and "surprising phenomena"
3-68. The purpose of the true spiritual formation by Self-completion
3-69. The principle of the relative original power based on the higher dimensional spirit and mind
3-70. Culture and civilization based on spiritual dimension
3-71. Energy waves in the seven spiritual dimensions
3-72. SHINSEI (true sense) is the common denominator of the entire universe
3-73. The relative original power with the high-dimensional being
3-74. Unpleasant feelings are caused by spiritual disorder
3-75. The way of life to integrate individual purpose and entire purpose
3-76. Create the path to manifest SHINSEI (true sense)
3-77. Advent of "the Eschatology" in Christianity and "the declining days of this world" in Buddhism
3-78. "The Eschatology" in Christianity and "the declining days of this world" in Buddhism, based on the view of religious history
3-79. The sacred revelation from the universe
3-80. Human being is a cancer cell of the terrestrial life entities
3-81. The relative wave and the relative original power based on mind and spirit

For more information please contact us :
Self-Healing Study and Practice Group
(info@selfhealing.co.in)

www.ingramcontent.com/pod-product-compliance
Lightning Source LLC
Chambersburg PA
CBHW050759160426
43192CB00010B/1576